For All The ░░░░

St. Michael's Church
East Peckham

Parish and People

by

Margaret Lawrence

Margaret Lawrence.

"For God is not unrighteous to forget your work and labour of love which you have shown towards his name in that you have ministered to the saints."
(Hebrews 6 v.10)

This publication is assisted by an award from the Allen Grove Local History Fund of the Kent Archaeological Society and by an award from the Kent History Fund of the same Society. Profits to the Churches Conservation Trust, for the Maintenance of St. Michael's Church.

Cover: The Valley Scene from St. Michael's Church. © Peter Street.

East Peckham lies between Maidstone and Tonbridge on the edge of the Weald. It is a large parish of some 3,400 acres with the River Medway flowing through the south. In recent years due to an expanding population a village centre was developed but historically the population was small and scattered among a series of hamlets. The present population is about 3,300.

St. Michael's church lies in an isolated position near the northern boundary, almost three miles from the modern centre. On approaching the church the visitor sees that it is set at the edge of a wood into a deep south-east slope just below the crest of a hill overlooking the Medway valley. It is positioned within a roughly circular churchyard at a height of 310 feet (95 metres). National Grid Reference TQ66385157

This book is 'for all the saints'; for the thousands of men and women over many centuries whose lives were influenced by St. Michael's church.

Acknowledgements

Geofrey Allibone, for translating the Twysden Monument from Latin. Alan Applegate for the map of medieval houses. Peter Batts, Friends of Kent Churches, for help with stained glass. Richard Cann, for photography at Baddesley Clinton. Chloe Cockerill, Churches Conservation Trust, for help with heraldry. Peter Cormack, William Morris Gallery for help with stained glass. CR Humphery-Smith, Institute Genealogical Studies Canterbury for Italian research. Howard Jones, Architectural Historian, for his survey of the church. Philip Lawrence, for his contribution on Monumental Brasses and for editing the text. Dickon Love, for permission to publish his web site of the bells of St. Michael's. Colin Rainer, for photography. David Sampson and SRS Graphics, for additional photography, design and layout of the book. Peter Street, for cover design. Joan Thirsk for continual interest and encouragement. B.C. Worssam, Geologist, for his study of the exterior building stone. To the staff, past and present, of the Centre for Kentish Studies.

References

To avoid over referencing throughout this book, please note the following:

1. Unless otherwise referenced, all Wills referred to were proved in the Prerogative Court of Canterbury. The references may be found on www.documentsonline.pro.gov.uk The Wills themselves can be downloaded. Also available for reference is www.kentarchaeology.org.uk the web site of the Kent Archaeological Society. This contains many transcripts of PCC wills from the notebooks of the antiquarian Leland Duncan (1862–1923).
2. Original Shoreham Deanery Wills and Inventories are held at Lambeth Palace Library. They are held on film at the Centre for Kentish Studies Maidstone.
3. The Churchwardens Presentments 1623–1761 are held at Lambeth Palace Library.
4. The Bishop's Visitation Records 1717, 1763, 1786, 1805 and 1864, are held at Lambeth Palace Library. That of 1758 has been published as the Speculum of Archbishop Thomas Secker. (edited Jeremy Gregory.) That of 1911 is recorded in the Church Vestry Book.

Abbreviations

AC	Archaeologia Cantiana, the annual volume of the Kent Archaeological Society.	KAL	Kent Archaeological Society Library.
BL	British Library.	LMA	London Metropolitan Archives.
CKS	Centre for Kentish Studies.	LPL	Lambeth Palace Library.
CCA	Canterbury Cathedral Archives.	NA	National Archives (formerly Public Record Office).
CRS	Catholic Record Society.		
DNB	Dictionary of National Biography.	SD	Shoreham Deanery.

Published by Margaret Lawrence.
Design and layout by David Sampson of SRS Graphics, Tunbridge Wells.
Printed by Geerings of Ashford Ltd.

ISBN 0 906746 60 4
© Margaret Lawrence 2004 unless otherwise credited.

Contents

Church Dedication

Saint Michael was looked to for spiritual defence. As a biblical figure he appears in the Book of Revelation when *'there was war in heaven and Michael and his angels fought against the dragon … and the great dragon, that old serpent called the Devil and Satan was cast out'*. (Revelations 12 v.7–12) Churches dedicated to St. Michael, such as the one in East Peckham, are most often found in a defensive position on high ground.

The medieval Christian sought his protection through prayer;

'God be favourable to me a sinner and be my guard all the days of my life … have mercy on me and send to my aid Michael your Archangel that he may keep protect and defend me from all my enemies, visible and invisible.'

Figure 1. St. Michael depicted in two ways – in armour treading down the devil, and, as the holder of a pair of scales for the weighing of souls. Barton Turf, Norfolk. © Richard Tilbrook. (By courtesy of Norfolk County Council Library and Information Services.)

'Holy Michael, the Archangel of God, defend me in battle that I may not perish in the dreadful judgement. Archangel of Christ, by the grace which you have merited I beseech you, through our only begotten Lord Jesus Christ, draw me today and always from deadly peril'.

Medieval Christians also found comfort in visual representations of the saint. As a symbol of God's power and providence St. Michael is depicted in two ways in medieval art; in armour, treading down the ancient enemy in the form of a serpent or dragon, and as the holder of a pair of giant scales for the weighing of souls because at the last day one's good deeds will be weighed in the balance against one's bad deeds. The devil tries to weigh down one side, urging sin, while the virgin intercedes with compassion by touching the other scale to weigh it down in favour of the soul. These images are found side by side. A notable example survives on the rood screen in the church at Barton Turf, Norfolk (Fig 1).

Churches dedicated to St. Michael are thought to be associated with the post Norman conquest period of church building. Pre-conquest dedications were often associated with Saxon saints such as St. Dunstan at West Peckham.

The evidence for an East Peckham Saxon church being strong it is possible that when the new Norman church was built it was rededicated in Norman tradition.

The Patronal Festival of St. Michael is September 29th. A commemorative service is still held at the church on the nearest Sunday to that date.

PART I

1. The Medieval Church and Parish

The Silent Witnesses

A hand solemnly placed on the altar of Christ Church Canterbury in 961 ensured East Peckham of a place in Saxon history. The hand was that of Ediva the Queen Mother, widow of Edward King of England and mother of Edmund and Edred, both in turn Kings of England. In the presence of all the King's bishops and prominent men she placed the deeds of her manor of Peckham, with those of seven other manors, on the altar dedicating them to the monks of Christ Church. In doing so a document was drawn up to prove her right of title to these lands of which she had previously been wrongfully deprived. This document reveals that her father was Sighelm, ealdorman of Kent who was responsible for organising the county militia and who was acclaimed by none other than King Alfred himself as *'his faithful warrior'*. Acting on a premonition that he would not return from battle against the Danes (902 at Holme in East Anglia) he bequeathed his lands in Kent to Ediva who must have been but a small child. It has previously been supposed that when Ediva gave her manor of Peckham to the monks in 961 there was a church on a Christian queen's manor.[1] Now the strong possibility is that there was a church on her father's manor in the preceding century on account of his high office and close association with that most Christian King Alfred.[2]

Although it was situated in the geographical Diocese ruled by the Bishop of Rochester the dedicated manor from that moment became the Archbishop of Canterbury's Peculiar (from the Latin 'to belong exclusively'). East Peckham was included in his Deanery of Shoreham.[3] This was to become a frustration for historians because the medieval records of the Archbishop's Peculiars which contain vital information have been lost.

That factual voice in 961 only briefly penetrates the silence and leaves many hundreds of years unaccounted for. How long had there been a settlement which came to be known as the 'ham on the peak', the settlement on the peak?[4] Other contextual evidence needs consideration.

It is generally accepted that many Christian churches were built on the sites of

Figure 2. Queen Ediva. A late representation of the Queen in Canterbury Cathedral. © Colin Rainer.

pagan religion. Indeed Pope Gregory instructed the future Bishop of London in 601 that not all pagan sacred places should be destroyed but rather that they should be sanctified with holy water and that Christian altars should be set up in them; so that in surroundings which already had powerful and familiar religious associations, the people would be more easily won to the new faith.

Those who wish to contemplate that the intriguing hill top site was thus associated can take into account that there is suggestive evidence of Iron Age occupation in the village area. The field name 'Speltland' found in documents of (1363) in the Beltring area was the name of corn grown in the Iron Age.[5] Undeniably there is evidence of the Iron Age tracks named 'spyche' associated with the Wealden iron industry. The name is found only in Essex and Kent. Made of brushwood, these were raised causeways laid across bog or flood lands to carry the iron out of the Weald.[6] East Peckham early documents contain such names as 'Gongspiche', 'Ferrinspiche', 'Buckspiche' as well as many corruptions of the word.[7] The position of the church is on one of the main Iron Age tracks out of the dense Wealden forest which crossed the five Medway ford crossings at what is now Branbridges. There were other fords through streams long since piped underground. The hill top site was also a resting place for the loaded haulage after the strenuous up hill climb and before the welcome descent. This commercial aspect could be included in any explanation of the site's origin.

However no archaeological evidence has yet been found for the four hundred years occupation by the Romans although their neighbours' farmhouses (villas) have been found at Teston, Barming, Wateringbury and Mereworth. It is the Jutish settlers who have left evidence of their presence and gave the place its name. They survived the many vicissitudes which passed over Kent having their effect on each local community.

After St Augustine arrived in Kent in 597 he organised his Christian mission efficiently by establishing 'mother churches' in influential areas from which preachers were sent to the surrounding villages. How soon did a Christian missionary arrive to found a church on the 'peak' and change the pagan way of life? Was he there in time to comfort the bereaved during the dynastic struggles in 685 when Caedwalla of Wessex laid waste Kent?

How large was the community and how many local men would have been called to serve in the Saxon army known as the Fyrd when later convulsions shook Kent in the ninth and tenth centuries as described in the Anglo Saxon Chronicle?

Did the missionary's successor comfort the people with prayers for protection from the fierce Danish invaders who raided Kent in the years following 835? The ancient petition, *'from the fury of the Northmen good Lord deliver us'*, may well have resounded on the peak. The massive incursion of Aethelwulf King of Wessex in 851 when he 'made the greatest slaughter of a heathen (Danish) host that we ever have heard tell of at Acleah' would have had repercussions here. A later Danish victory at Rochester in 999 gave them possession of a large number of horses. *'The Danes rode far and wide as they pleased destroying and laying waste almost the whole of West Kent'.* The subsequent payment of tribute to the Northmen in 1002 would certainly have required local contributions. Of all these violent disturbances there is no direct evidence of their effect on East Peckham. But the larger unit of which it was part was clearly subject to a series of spasms of major importance.

How soon was the valley tilled? Many ideas have been offered to explain why the parish church of St. Michael stands high on the hill remote from the village below. It has been said that the hill top village was destroyed by the Black Death of the fourteenth century and rebuilt in the valley below, that it was a village which gradually slid down hill as conditions in the valley improved and that it was a village which developed on the banks of the Medway when the Medway Navigation Company built its wharf there in 1740.

In fact none of these ideas have any substance. Further settlement in the valley developed long before the Norman conquest. The evidence lies in the Domesday survey of 1086, the first 'market research' survey when King William I in order to assess that he was receiving adequate taxes sent his Commissioners countrywide to record what each manor was worth before the Conquest and what it was then worth 20 years later. Historians interpreting the Peckham entry have found that in contrast to the rest of the Weald, it was an old established community fully organised into boroughs and manors with roughly 2,120 acres under cultivation.[8] There is further evidence of an outstanding property, a Saxon royal manor of sixty acres, (Burrs Oak Farm) and another holding of sixty acres held by King William's half brother, the powerful Bishop of Bayeux (Newerk in the Bush area).[9] Also recorded is the manorial mill which later manorial documents prove to be that at Branbridges on the Medway.[10]

Further pointers to the early occupation of the valley lie in the field names found in medieval documents. Names such as Wolueren – Woolfreeds – Horsongy – Dralathe – le Sikey Sikere – Le Watchell, Estropysstane, speak of men who tilled the soil of the valley and spoke the names maybe even before they were written down. These names are possibly of Saxon origin.

A still apparent indication of life in the valley is the antiquity of its timber framed houses. The recent survey of medieval houses in Kent recorded 22 existing medieval houses dating from before 1550 in East Peckham and a further 6 have been discovered making a total of 28, the earliest estimated at c1350.[11] However these houses were themselves replacements of earlier houses with their ancient associated land holdings. In addition many documents record where an *ancient messuage formerly stood*. The map indicates where there is documentary evidence for an earlier house together with those existing today. This shows the spread of the medieval population in relation to the position of the church.

To what building did the people flee when the disastrous news of defeat came from Hastings in 1066? Was it the church building recorded in the Domesday survey? The implied eruption of an alien hierarchy with its administrative patterns and values can be readily imagined. The survey recorded an 'ecclesia' here indicating that there was a consecrated church. Another source, the Domesday Monachorum, the records of Christchurch Canterbury, records that Peckham paid a chrism fee to the bishop of Rochester for the blessed oil used in baptism, further evidence for an active consecrated church. Did the ten slaves recorded in the Domesday book ever look to the building on the hill for spiritual comfort? It is a provoking thought that the eleventh century congregation of Saxon ceorls and bondsmen joined with the intruded Norman landholders in the unity of the Mass.

Who were the people who watched the metamorphosis of that earlier church? Perhaps the parents of Richard de Stanford who conducted a land dispute in 1163 would have been witnesses and passed the story down through their family who were to live here for another six hundred years.[12] Certainly, Benedict of Wodeshale would have seen more by 1259. His house is mentioned when a cavalcade of twelve horsemen appointed by the Archbishop of Canterbury and twelve horsemen appointed by Richard Earl of Gloucester and Hereford, of Tonbridge Castle made a perambulation to settle a boundary dispute in that year. When they came to one point on the

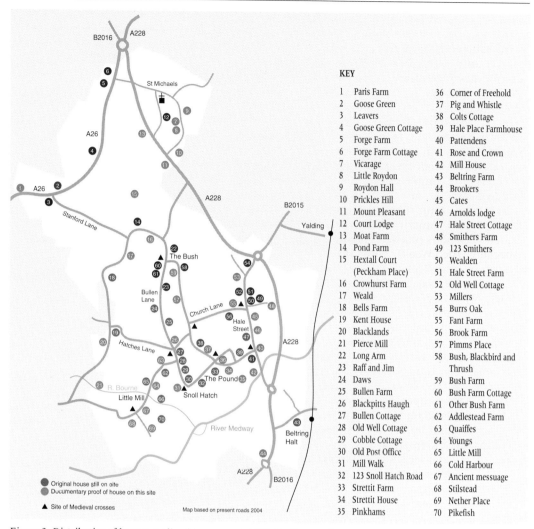

Original house still on site
Documentary proof of house on this site

▲ Site of Medieval crosses   Map based on present roads 2004

Figure 3. Distribution of known medieval houses as at 1550. © Alan Applegate

boundary of Hadlow and East Peckham they recorded the house of Benedict as being on the archbishop's land in East Peckham.[13] The exact spot is known because the house, rebuilt over the years, kept its name, corrupted from Wodeshale to Woodsalls until 1785 when William Paris took the lease of the farm thereafter known to this day by his name.[14] By that date of 1259 the scaffolding was surely erected at the church and Roger de Syssinghurst and John de Leicester are respectively the first recorded rector and vicar in 1287. Were these the first resident clergy under the Norman bureaucracy or merely the first to be recorded? By 1336 when Alice de Stanford buried her chaplain John de Ardenne *'feloniously killed in her own house at Goose Green by John at Weld, John his son and Roger le Rook,'* the church must have been very much of the shape and size as shown on the plan of the mid 13th century church.[15]

The families who had watched the church developing on the hill and perhaps even helped to build it were those who went to the church to bury their dead during the years of the Black Death. The peak year of the plague was 1346 when it is estimated that in some areas one third of the population died and in others as many as half of the population. Although evidence for

East Peckham is lacking there is no reason to suppose that it fared differently from the rest of the country. Possibly William Bansor may have been officiating at the church at this time. Certainly later in 1400 and 1426 William Milton, John Wyke, Richard Ecclesley, and John Smale were all recorded as rectors.[16] Although their building was probably complete were they troubled by the new preaching initiated by John Wycliffe that opposed so many of the church's religious practices? Kent, especially the Weald with the

Figure 4. Bullen Cottage. An obvious medieval house. © Colin Rainer.

Maidstone and Rochester areas, was later to be a stronghold for Wycliffe's followers who became known as Lollards (a word derived from mumblers, preachers). They were people who were prepared to die for their beliefs. They denied that Christ was physically present in the bread and wine at the Eucharist, that oral confession to a priest was misdirected since only God could forgive sin, and that praying to images and making pilgrimages was unnecessary. All was based on the startling fact that the Bible had for the first time been translated from Latin into the mother tongue. This 'heresy', as it was defined by ecclesiastical authority, was carried by travellers and seemed to have appealed especially to artisans, weavers, tailors and the like.

What did William Hextal of Hextall Court (Peckham Place) see in 1450 as he rode up hill from his home together with a band of East Peckham men to join his fellow Kentish men in a revolt against the King led by Kentish Jack Cade? Did Hextal see the scaffolding on the south side of the church as the wall was disturbed by the insertion of new windows. Was the mason who left his marks on the inner work a local man? Were William and his fellows of the East Peckham contingent resentful at seeing the wealth of the parish going to the upkeep of monks at Christchurch, Canterbury? The regular visits of the monk-wardens to collect rents from local farmers must surely have been an irritant to men whose demands were that church estates should be confiscated and the land distributed among the people who worked it.

William was very fortunate ever to see the church of the late 15th century (on plan) again because although the revolt failed both he and John Hubble of East Peckham were given the royal pardon and escaped the death penalty which was the fate of many others.

William's father Richard Hextal had come from an estate in Staffordshire to East Peckham towards the end of the reign of Richard II (1377–1399) and through marriage increased his lands both locally and in East Kent around Dover. While little is

Figure 5. Addlestead Farm. Internally retains a medieval house. © Colin Rainer.

known about Richard's prior career that of William shows him to have been a man of some substance. He inherited the Hextall lands in Kent and lands in Warwickshire and Staffordshire and was sub sheriff of that latter county; he was commissioner of array, responsible for recruiting archers, procuring ships and for musters of soldiers; he was a tax collector; he was escheator of Staffordshire and Kent overseeing the estates of those who died without heirs or with an under age heir, to ensure that the estate reverted to the lord of the manor or to the King; he was a Teller of the Exchequer; he was one of the keepers of the temporalities of the archbishopric of Canterbury (those ecclesiastical holdings subject to secular control) and he was a member of the Great Council of 1455, (closest advisers to the King.)[17] Important locally is the fact that he was attorney and adviser to Humphrey Stafford 1st Duke of Buckingham, Lord of Tonbridge Castle and it is probable that the Hextalls came from Stafford initially in the service of the castle household and were granted lands in East Peckham, probably those originally granted by King William to Richard of Tonbridge at the conquest, as recorded in the Domesday entry.

It was usual among the gentry at that time to establish themselves in a community by becoming patrons of the local church and it is conceivable that it was he who funded the three newer style perpendicular windows in the south aisle and established a family Lady Chapel and burial place there.

Those who watched the building change and grow over these centuries into its present shape also worshipped within these walls. They are the earliest named witnesses but soon the silence of history is to be relieved by further documentary evidence.

References

1 Margaret Lawrence. 'Through This Door' 1973.
2 AC vol 36 The Picture of Queen Ediva in Canterbury Cathedral.
3 I. Churchill. Canterbury Administration.
4 J.K.Wallenburg. Kentish Place Names.
5 CKS U754 T7 1386 Speltland.
6 K.Witney. The Jutish Forest 1976.
7 CKS U1115 T59-Gongspiche 1375. U745 T7-Ferringspiche 1386. U282 T60-Buckspiche 1549.
8 Darby and Campbell. Geography of South Eastern England 1968.
9 AC v 98 M Lawrence. A Saxon Royal Manor.
10 CCA Ancient Charters P13 1478. Lease of Branbridge Mill.
11 S. Pearson. Medieval Houses of Kent. An Historical Analysis. Published Royal Commission on Historical Monuments 1994.
12 CKS U38 E2 and AC vol 72 Dumbreck. The Lowy of Tonbridge.
13 CKS U119 T13 A Capital Messuage called Woodsalls.
14 Calendar Inquisitions Misc. File 1305.
15 See later, Monumental Brasses.
16 CH Fielding. Records of the Rochester Diocese. 1910.
17 JC Wedgewood. History of Parliament.

The Voice of the Witnesses

It is in the 15th century that direct information about the church becomes available and makes possible a backward look to decipher how the church has developed.

To this church came the medieval population of East Peckham. Many of their names flash briefly in manorial rentals and legal documents and are heard of no more. Others in dying left in their testamentary records a living picture of their church, their faith and the society they lived in.

Such a one was John Cayser who died in 1491. By his request he was buried in the body of the church of St. Michael the Archangel. He arranged in his will to leave 3s.4d to the High Altar to ease his conscience in case he had forgotten or neglected to pay his tithe owing to the church. This was essential because failure to pay one tenth of all his produce could result in excommunication and, it was believed, consequent separation from God. He also took further precautions for the well being of his soul by ensuring that he would be remembered in his church. This was because evidence of his generosity would remind people to pray for him. Therefore he provides for the wall painting of the image of our Lady of Pity, 6s.8d (that of Mary supporting the dead Christ) and for the amending and painting of the images of St. Michael and Saint Nicholas. He arranges for the *'reparacions'* of the High Altar and repairs and *'guildes'* the cross and repairs the window dedicated to Saint Blaise. For some reason he thought to provide for the construction of an east and north window in the steeple. Furthermore he instructs his executor to buy a chalice of the value of 40s for use in God's divine service and also to make a chest in which to put the goods of East Peckham.

Most of this work vanished with the austerity of the later Reformation but his main glory remains, namely that of *'to the making of the south window of the said church'*. Now of plain glass the original would have been coloured medieval glass. Fragments of medieval glass can be seen in the north window above the pulpit and in a window in the south aisle. He shows the religious belief of the time by providing for a yearly obit (a mass on the anniversary of his death) in the church *'for the health of his soul, Johanne his wife's soul, John Cayser's soul, Johan Cayser's soul, Robert Cayser and Alice his wife's, all his parents' souls and all true Christian souls'*. This was on account of their fear of Purgatory and their belief that prayers after death could ease the way through their torment.

John Cayser was clearly a man of means. He had inherited property from his father Robert. He was Lord of the Manor of Caysers, previously known as Lomewood, which meant that he owned property which was subject to the obligations and customs of manorial life. Details of his personal life are evident from his domestic bequests. He arranges for his wife to be cared for in the customary manner of the time. She was to have her *'easement'* and occupation of a chamber in the south end of his messuage in which he then dwelt (and no doubt where these words were being penned,) with *'fire and fleet'* in the hall with free coming and going. Also she was to have a piece of land on which she was to have the profit from growing flax and hemp.

This detailed picture of a family who worshipped in this church is enhanced by

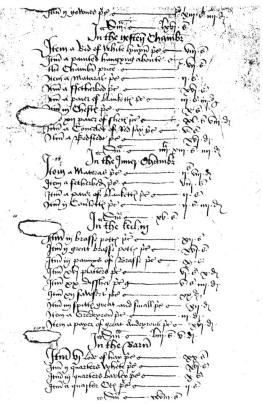

Figure 6. Inventory of John Cayser 1491 showing details of the guest chamber, the inner chamber and the kitchen. (By permission of National Archives PROB 2/47.)

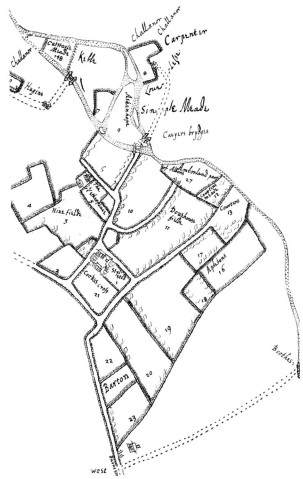

Figure 7. Twysden Estate Map 1632. This shows the original Stilstead farm site. The road, which branched off to Caysers bridge, was originally the Kings Highway and continued (off map) to the Bourne and to Snoll Hatch. The latter section is now a public footpath. (Add Ms 34155 by permission of the British Library.)

John's probate inventory. This in itself is of great interest because probate inventories for this period are rare and moreover this is the second earliest Kent example preserved in the Prerogative Court of Canterbury records in the National Archives. It is in good condition and a pleasure to read.[1]

His house may have been a very early example of a timber framed house type. Because no upstairs rooms are indicated it may have been all on one floor. The hall was certainly open to the timber roof. It was the living area and furnished with two tables and two forms. John, the master of the house sat at one of these tables with the wall behind him hung with an *'old painted cloth'*. Eight silver spoons and a maser could be seen by the assessor as well as eight bacon hoggs in the roof no doubt curing as the smoke rose from the open fire on the hall floor.

The parlour, his private room where he slept with his wife Johan was hung with a better quality painted hanging and contained a bedstead with a mattress and a feather bed, a pair of blankets and *'a coverlette for a gentlewoman'*. It was furnished with a form and a chest and visible were two doublets, two pairs of hose and two gowns.

In the guest chamber was a bed of white linen and, a luxury item for privacy of toilet, *'a painted hanging around the chamber piece'*. The bedstead, mattress, feather bed and a pair of blankets were topped by a coverlette of red say, (a cloth of fine texture). There were three chests and twelve pairs of sheets.

In the inner chamber no bedstead was provided. Apparently when sleeping on the floor someone was glad of a mattress, feather bed, a pair of blankets and a coverlette.

In the kitchen, which may have been a separate outside building, there were *'three brass pots, two great brass pots, three pans of brass, sixteen platters, twenty dishes, four spitts great and small, two gridirons, a pair of great andirons'* supporting the wood on the fire.

In the barn he had *'six loads of hay, two quarters of wheat, three quarters of barley, and a quarter of oats. In the farmyard two carts and a plough, six capons, ten hens and sixteen chicken. In cattle six oxen, sixteen hogs, two boars and two horses.'* The total value of his possessions came to £56.2s.10d which included money owed to him from the sale of oxen.

As interesting and as informative a picture as this is it does not tell the whole story. The assessors were only required to record the money in his purse, moveable chattels and debts due. Real property was not required. John bequeathed his real property to his son William and it is not until 1510 that three properties are named in William's will as *'all that capital mansion house of Stylsted, also Adylsies, and Quaifes'*. The first two names are recognised today as Stilstead and Addlestead – the last property stood opposite Addlestead.

The two documents show a family which has overcome the aftermath of the Black Death when farmers had to realise that new methods of agriculture were needed to adapt to a much smaller population. They have adapted to and are gaining profit from the newer crops of flax and hemp and have a thriving pig industry with pigs and boars in the farmyard and bacon joints smoking in the hall using the smoke rising from the open fireplace and there is money owed to him from the sale of cattle. The Twysden estate map 1632 shows the exact position of the Cayser's house and the route of an old road which met a T junction with the Tonbridge road.[2] In recent years this has been used as an entry road to new development The archaeology of the old road and farmstead can still be seen when the field is ploughed. The house remained updated and modernised according to the fashions of the centuries until it was demolished in 1844 to be replaced by the re-sited present brick farmhouse slightly to the south east.[3] Conversely part of the medieval Adylsies remains within the present Addlestead farmhouse.

Other testamentary records add to the lay out of the medieval church. Earlier in 1420 John Mew asked to be buried within the church in the chancel of the Blessed Virgin Mary, Mother of God, and second only to Christ himself in the vocabulary of worship. This is now referred to as the Twysden chapel. Sir Henry Ferrers 1500, second husband of Margaret Hextall (daughter of William Hextal above) refers to the family burial place when he asked to be buried in our Lady Chapel next to his wife. Walter Walsh Vicar 1515 asked to be buried in the sanctuary. Joanne Waller asked to be buried in the chancel of the Blessed Lady.[4] Walter Walshe also provided money for the light on the rood beam as did Robert Thetcher 1528.

John A Downe of Beltring 1542 requested burial directly before the high altar which stood within the chancel thus allowing room for processions to pass around it (not against the east wall).

More scenes from the medieval church can be envisaged through these testamentary records. William Byrch 1474 records a statue to Saint Blaise. William Cayser 1510 reveals the existence of three more statues leaving money for the light of St. Mary, and the light of St. Michael the Archangel (which stood presumably on the base by the north door) as well as the light before the image of our Lady of Grace. Walter Walsh mentions the light of the Blessed Mary which stood within the door of the church. This completes the total of seven statues which find mention.

The adornment of the church is also portrayed. John Mew clearly felt a responsibility to the church. *'I give to the fabric of the chancel of the Virgin Mary in the church of East Peckham £10'* and to those who ministered there he gave one missal, one vestment and one chalice. Was he preparing a resting place for the final adornment of his own knightly monumental brass of which now only the indent remains? Richard Etclesley who must have worshipped with him, also left money for the church fabric and he too was remembered for many years until his monumental brass was removed.[5]

Ralph Brooks 1507 provided for *'the binding of the books pertaining to the said church'*.

The outside of the church featured in bequests which provides vital information. Richard Peckerill 1452[6] with a practical gesture, provides a sum for the church roof and Ralph Broke in leaving money for the *'shingling of the church'* shows that it was roofed with flat wooden tiles. His bequest to the church porch probably means that the present porch had been added by that date. No one mentions the upkeep of the churchyard but there are frequent requests to be buried there.

The testamentary records also breathe the atmosphere of the church by frequent reference to the music for the dead. Mass was chanted on the third, seventh and thirtieth days following burial and on the first anniversary, the *'obit'*. There could also be an annual *'years mind'* which could extend for many years if financially provided for. Another memorial was the *'trental'* which was thirty masses celebrated on thirty consecutive days at the 'weeks mind'. On these anniversaries the deceased would be present symbolically in the form of a draped hearse surrounded by candles. The church was alive with the sound and movement of these observances and some testaments picture the number of staff required to fulfil its numerous tasks. John Mew mentions the Sacrist and the Clerk, besides which records show that he had his own domestic chaplain. After numerous bequests he arranged for three thousand masses to be said for his soul and his wives' souls and for all the faithful deceased to be paid for from the sale of his substantial property in East Peckham, Wateringbury and Tudely. Richard Peckerill left money for masses to be celebrated for his soul and Robert Thetcher for an honest secular priest (non regular clergy) to sing a trental of masses. Ralph Broker left money for ten priests to sing *'for his soul on the day of his obit and at his months mynd'* and a further sum for twenty years and mentions Sir Hugh, chantry priest. He was a priest employed solely to chant masses for the dead. The title 'Sir', was a a normal term of respect. Richard Hoggyn 1490 also asked for a secular priest, to sing and read in the said church of East Peckham for my soul *'the space of a whole year'*.

Joanne Waller paid for a priest to sing mass for her soul, her husband's soul and all her children's souls in the church of East Peckham for two years after her decease. She also made arrangements for her funeral which again required music. Her request to be buried within the church of East Peckham was complicated by the fact that although born to the Whetenhall family at Hextal she lived in West Malling. She arranged to pay eight people 12d each for their labour to carry her body for burial and to pay four men 4d each to carry torches to her burial. Four priests were paid 12d each to accompany her body for burial and those who attended both Dirige and Mass at her burial 12d each but if they only attended Mass 8d each. She further made arrangements for thirty Masses.

John Cayser's wife Johane was also buried within the church as ascertained by her son William 1510, who asked to be buried in the church *'prope matrem mea'*, next to my mother.

The influence of the medieval church spread literally to every corner of the village. This is why the history of the church must not be confined to a mere history of the building but to the people, their lives and the village they lived in.

Thus John Cayser reveals yet another aspect of the medieval church. Although a neighbour, William Byrche dying earlier raises a question by bequeathing money for the upkeep of the cross called Stone Cross, John Cayser leaves no doubt as to the purpose of the cross; he leaves money for a shaft for the *crucifix* at Stone Cross (Stone Pitt on the Tonbridge Road).

These 'stone' clues at junctions of the village roads were marked by wayside shrines so that at every turning people were reminded of the influence of the church. The shrines seem to be placed at Tee junctions, almost like signposts, leaving us mistakenly to assume that there was once a series of cross roads. As well as the Stone Cross probably at the tee junction shown on the Twysden map 1632 there is ample evidence from documents that there were Crosses at:

Chidley Cross, 1556 *'lying to the Queen's highway leading from Hale Street to Chitley Cross'* (junction Pound Road and Chidley Cross Roads.)[7]

Blackpitt Cross, 1556 *'iacet ad regia via ducem … Blackpitts cross'* lying to the King's way leading to Blackpitts Cross. (junction Addlestead Road and Tonbridge Road)[8]

Strodette Cross, 1524 *'to the repair of Strodette Cross'* (junction Snoll Hatch Road and Pound Road[9]

Pattendens Cross, 1542, *'half an acre lying to Patenden's land against the Crosse.'* (junction Old Road and Hale Street)[10]

Snode Hatch, 1569, where a property is described as *'iaciens apud Snode Hatch in East Peckham ad crucem'* – lying at Snode Hatch in East Peckham at the cross. (junction of Kings highway, now footpath, to Little Mill and Addlestead Road.[11]

Newerke Cross, 1556, *'unum messauge apud Newereke Cross'* – one messuage at Newerke Cross. (junction of Bush Road and Bullen Lane.[12]

Hale Cross or **Hale Crouch**, 1380, *'near the cross called Hale Cross sometimes called Hale Crouch'*.[13] This is the most frequently mentioned because it was a Borough meeting place. Most likely junction of Hale street and Smithers Lane. William Hextal writing in about 1450 to the Archbishop of Canterbury begged him on behalf of his tenants of the Borough of Stockenbury to allow their law day *'to be holden at the said place of olde tyme accustomed called the Hale cross'* rather than changing it to Farleigh, five miles distance.[14]

Messengers Cross, 1482, *'on the way from Hale Cross to Messengers Cross'*,[15] No proof of site.

This also shows that the present pattern of the village lanes was already well established.

The church community reached out to the poor. Some like Richard Hugelet although buried at Maidstone in 1404 remembered the paupers of Peckham in his will. John Mew also left a generous sum of 100 shillings to *'the most needy of the poor'* and Richard Peckeryll although not so wealthy was mindful to leave a smaller mount. But John Cayser was more specific. *'I will that every Good Friday during the term of three years that my executors to distribute for the health of my soul to the poor people 10s. I will 5s worth of herrings be distributed yearly to the poor people during the term of three years upon the first Sunday in clear Lent.'* Also unusual was Richard Hoggyn's provision of money to *'the marriage of poor maidens'*. Joanne Waller, left the poor people money for bread and drink on the day of her burial and further money to be kept for bread and drink on her anniversaries for two years.

There are few references to the ordinary medieval man who was baptised, married, attended mass in St. Michael's church and was buried in its churchyard before the parish registers were begun. But in 1449 a property was sold to Gilbert Pertrych and Margary his wife on condition that *'they find William Rolfe and Alice his wife in food and drink and for the next six years to find them one pair of stockings and one pair of socks and after six years to find them woolen clothes annually for their lives; viz to William one year a coat and the next a tunic and to Alice in like manner one year a gown and the other year a kirtle. Also after the said six years to find the said William and Alice for life in woolen clothes, shoes and bedding with reasonable washing'*. Provision was also made for their peaceable accommodation within the house and a herb garden without. Nothing more is known about William and Alice except for the sure picture that they were warm in church in their woollen clothes and clean stockings and socks.[16]

One disappointment in the testamentary records is that Willaim Grocyn with his love of education did not mention East Peckham in his lengthy will. He was the great scholar known as the patriarch of English learning who had enthused the educated world by way of the universities of Europe with his love of the Greek manuscripts so recently discovered in the sacked libraries of Constantinople and had introduced the study of Greek to Oxford University. Much admired and loved by Renaissance scholars, Erasmus, Linacre and others, he was by 1511 a sick man suffering from paralysis and was given the Mastership of the Priest's College at Maidstone for retirement and was also appointed Rector of East Peckham. He is said to have spent his revenues on lavish hospitality but in the years before his death in 1519 there is no sign that gave a thought to East Peckham except by appointing a vicar as he was required to do.[17]

As a finale to medieval East Peckham Ralph Broker indicates the changing social life by the insertion of chimneys into the old houses and the flooring over of the open halls. He charges his wife *to have my chamber lofted and builded upon*. As some of the more prosperous of the population adapted to the luxury of fireplaces and smokeless houses even more dramatic changes were to follow in their church, their faith and the society they lived in.

References

1   NA Prob 2/47 With thanks to Gillian Rickard's work on researching the PCC Kentish Inventories.
2   BL Add Ms 34155 Twysden estate maps.
3   CKS U82 T357 'All that messuage called or known by the name of Stilstead'.
4   Rochester Wills. Joanne Waller.
5   See later Monumental Brasses.
6   Rochester wills Richard Peckerell.
7   CKS U48 T13.
8   Rochester Wills. Richard Peckerell.
9   Rochester Wills. John Erkenbold.
10 Will of John Down of Beltring.
11 CKS U47 M34 Manor of Albans.
12 BL Add Ms 34154 Manor of Eastmere 1566.
13 CKS U1823/105 Z31 Lambert Larking papers.
14 CCa DCc Canterbury Letters 6.
15 CKS U52 T49.
16 CKS U1823/105 Z31, notebook 7, P21 1449.
17 DNB Grocyn. His will is PCC but has been printed in Collectania II (Oxford Historical Society 1890).

2. The Tudor Parish

Within view of the church worshippers watched the drama of the new age of building. Roydon Hall was the first brick built house in East Peckham. Thomas Roydon, of an armigerous East Anglian family, came to Kent about 1500 and bought a small house called Fortune which he rebuilt and enlarged. How long it took to build from the plans and the foundation can only be conjectured but its completion in 1535 was obviously a cause for pride. '*Domus ista fuit edita 1535*' is proclaimed above the entrance, '*This house was built in 1535*'. He had married Margaret Whetenhall daughter of William Whetenhall and through the marriage of their daughter Elizabeth to her first husband, the Kentish Gentleman William Twysden, the property came into that family.[1]

He could not have understood how significant that date was to register in national history and in particular to the history of East Peckham and its church. It was only in the previous year 1534 that Henry VIII had declared himself to be Supreme Head of the Church in England abolishing the Pope's power in England and thus breaking the thousand year link with the Catholic Church. That was when the apparent change in the medieval church began but in fact it is considered that mens' thoughts were well prepared for the new way because of the incidence of well established Lollardy. This was particularly so in Kent where Lollards, the followers of Wycliffe, had been actively preaching in wealden towns and villages since the mid fifteenth century. Wycliffe's preachers were inspired by the newly translated Bible – from Latin to English – and Wycliffe himself shocked the established church by daring to quote from it to question some of its basic doctrines and practices. These mainly concerned the nature of the Eucharist, confession to a priest, the availability of scripture in the vernacular and the dislike of images and pilgrimages.

Although no Lollards are recorded by name in East Peckham other records show that they are known to have been preaching in the neighbouring villages of Marden, Hadlow, Yalding, and Brenchley as well as in the nearby towns of West Malling and Maidstone. This indicates a wide local awareness of their preaching.[2]

What happened at St. Michael's church in the following years was witnessed by the Whetenhall family. They were the principal land owners in the parish having inherited the Hextal estate in east and west Kent through the marriage about 1460 of William Whetenhall to Margaret Hextal sole heir of her father, the eminent William Hextal. As a young widow Margaret later made a prestigious marriage to Sir Henry Ferrers, of Hambleton in the County of Rutland, grandson of Baron Groby and had sons by him. It is highly probable that the children were born at Hextal and baptised at St. Michael's for their father was Sheriff of Kent in 1464 and again in 1483 and was Member of Parliament in 1472. Through his later marriage Sir Edward their eldest son inherited Baddesley Clinton in Warwickshire, the medieval moated manor house now owned by the National Trust where the names of his parents with their heraldic shields are displayed in the window glass of

the dining room They are also recorded on their son's altar tomb in the chancel of the neighbouring Baddesley Clinton Church. It reads:

'Here lieth Sir Edward Ferrers Knight son and heir of Sir Henry Ferrers and Margaret Hekstall his wife of East Peckham in the county of Kent knight. He died xx1x day of August 1535 leaving issue Henry Edward George and Nicholas'.

Figure 8. The familiar north front of Roydon Hall showing Thomas Roydon's original work – the Tudor entrance. The exterior of the house, as seen behind, belongs to a later architectural style. (By permission of the Spiritual Regeneration Movement of Great Britain)

Edward himself is portrayed in the stained glass east window of that church, wearing his heraldic costume, kneeling in prayer and surrounded by his family. This standard of living (or dying!) surely suggests an equivalent family status at St. Michael's. Possibly Sir Henry Ferrers' previous reference to his burial in *'our Lady Chapel'* refers to a Hextal chapel at the east end of the south aisle where architect Howard Jones dates the piscina c.1350. This is roughly the date when the Hextals are thought to have arrived in East Peckham.

But although Edward was Sir Henry's heir the Hextal estate reverted on his mother's death to William Whetenhall the son of her first marriage.

Edward Ferrer's long will of 1535 clearly shows his East Peckham and other local connections. He owned land in his own right and mentioned local people.

The Whetenhall's inherited home at Hextal Court was the principal house in the parish before Roydon Hall was built and must have been a substantial building. It is recorded on the later Hearth Tax Assessment of 1665 as a house with thirteen chimneys and was later, in 1780, described by Hasted, the Kentish historian, as *'venerable for its antiquity and was the mansion of gentlemen of that name'*. Considering the prestigious marriages, then and to come in the future, the house could well have been a quality medieval stone built house.

This very influential family was descended from an ancient armigerous lineage seated at Whetenhall near Chester who had seen service with the Black Prince. Among many other offices William's father, William Whetenhall (died 1456), was a citizen and alderman of the City of London, Warden of the Grocer's Company, Sheriff of London and Sergeant of the King's cellar.

Figure 9. Sir Edward Ferrer's tomb recording that he was the son of Sir Henry Ferrers and Margaret Hextall of East Peckham. Baddesley Clinton Church, Warwickshire. © Richard Cann.

The importance of this remarkable breed has been overshadowed by the social and political history of the later Twysden family of Roydon Hall which has been so carefully recorded by Sir Roger Twysden and others of his family but this family were not living in the parish during the vital years of the reformation. It is through the Whetenhall family more than any other that the whole range of religious history over two hundred years can be perceived. It was a spiritual story that led to their repression and eventually to the loss of their ancient inheritance.

William Whetenhall, dying in 1539, had been Sheriff of Kent, Justice of the Peace and tax collector. He was the last of the family whose will reflects the medieval usage. He shows that he was perfectly prepared for death and that his conscience was clear by having made arrangements which would avoid work for his executors. *'I minded to pay all my debts and bestowed for the health of my soul with mine own hand in my life time'*. He

Figure 10. Detail from east window, Baddesley Clinton Church, Warwickshire. Sir Edward surrounded by his family kneels at prayer wearing heraldic costume. © Richard Cann.

arranged for an honest month's mind to be kept for the health of his soul, for all true Christian souls, and to be buried next to his wife in the chapel called the chapel of Our Lady in the church of East Peckham.

It is surprising then to find that his son George who inherited his estate *'with all my goods, corn, grain and cattle'* and who became a leader in the community is found among those who accepted the new changes readily. It is thought that as a student at Cambridge he became influenced by the early Protestant movement through his association with Thomas Becon who later became a prominent Protestant reformer and writer and dedicated one of his works to his friend George Whetenhall. Becon and possibly George Whetenhall himself studied under Hugh Latimer later to become a Protestant Martyr. Such background is significant because this early influence upon Whetenhall as the principal landowner was a powerful factor in determining the future puritanical tone for the church in East Peckham.

King Henry remained a professed Catholic and changes in the churches were slow. Initially his concern was to assess his new income. The income from the church was derived from its local farming activity. The 'first fruits' of every benefice which had formerly been paid to the Pope together with a tenth of the annual income were now appropriated to the Crown. He commissioned the great Valor Ecclesiasticus which recorded the valuation of church and monastic properties throughout the land. For East Peckham the entry reads that the Rectory was valued at £23 and paid £2.6s in yearly 'tenths'. The vicarage was valued at £14 and paid £1.0s.8d yearly rates. This highlights the unusual fact that East Peckham retained both a rectory and a vicarage and had both ministers resident.[3]

Another concern was church administration and the need to establish it under his 'New Management'. The first act of the Reformation to affect St. Michaels, one which George Whetenhall would have heartily approved, was the 1540 dissolution of Christchurch monastery at Canterbury to which the manor and church belonged. This freed the rectorship from ecclesiastical ownership, vesting it in the Crown to be leased to a layman. It also released the church from monastic patronage and it was then placed in the hand of the Dean and Chapter of Canterbury a newly formed administration of non 'religious' people. From this point a pattern of Tithe was established which was to affect the church for hundreds of years.

The Great Tithes, a tenth of the crops, which had previously been claimed by the Rector now belonged to the lay lessee of the Rectory. These included the crops which grew from the ground – hay, corn, wood, fruit and herbs. It also included the responsibility for the upkeep of the chancel of the church.

The Small Tithes continued, as by custom, to be the perquisite of the Vicar. These included the non cereal items – that which was nourished from the earth – new born colts, calves, pigs, lambs, wool, chicken, eggs, honey, milk and butter.

Parish registers were another administrative innovation. Before 1538 there were no records of birth, deaths and marriages. Such events that might be needed for legal purposes would be remembered by word of mouth or by association with another event. The birth of William Whetenhall in 1468 was remembered by the fact that he was born on the day that his father died.[4] In small communities lack of information could lead to marriages not consistent with the laws of consanguinity. In 1538 every parson, vicar or curate received instructions that they were to enter in a book every wedding, christening and burial in his parish with the names of the parties. The St. Michael's registers survive from 1558, a later date, when entries on vellum were ordered. On September 7, 1558, Thomas Baker's name was the first to be written in the book. It was possibly the first time his name had ever been written down!

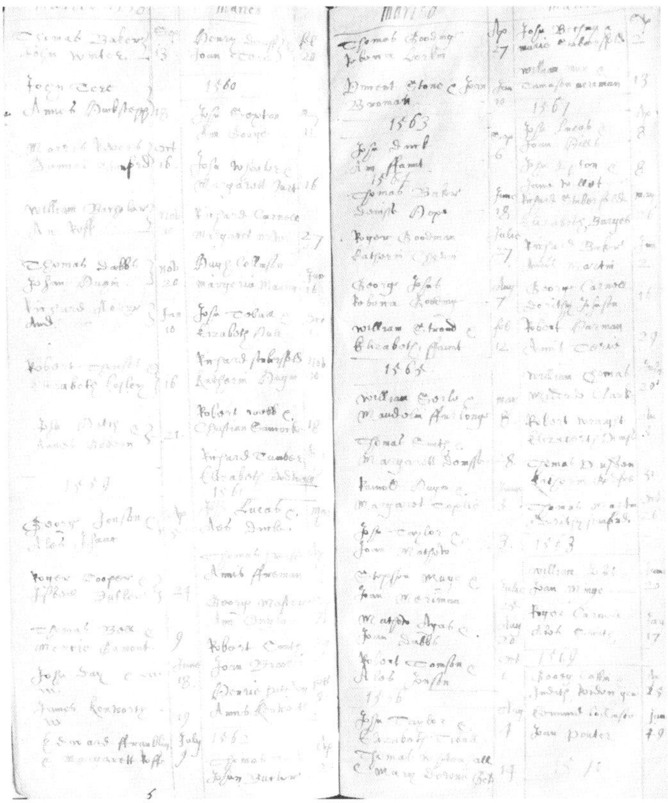

Figure 11. First page of Parish Marriage Registers – begun October 13th, 1558 (with permission of the Centre for Kentish Studies).

The small reforms Henry made within the church were also of a practical nature. He reduced the number of holy days and ceremonies because frequency of holidays and absenteeism from work was affecting trade and thus the economy and he banned the vogue for frequent pilgrimages on the same premise. Long standing scandals such as the sale of Indulgences, which fundamentally taught that forgiveness of sin could be purchased, were forbidden. The sale of supposed holy relics was banned as was the veneration of the saints. But the only positive contribution to spiritual welfare was the requirement that the faith should be taught for the first time in English and that the newly translated English Bible should be read in church.

For the reformers in the church and those such as George Whetenhall in the county there was disappointment concerning the fundamental doctrines of the faith. Henry made very few changes and traditional ceremonies and services continued unchanged. It has been said that the fabric of medieval religion remained torn and faded by fifteen years of attrition.[5]

Thus when Edward VI succeeded to the throne in 1547 St. Michael's was still a medieval church in appearance and the Mass was still in the Latin tongue.

The whole liturgical cycle was centred on the traditional mass culminating in the climax of the year with the celebration of the Easter Mass. On Good Friday the congregation took part in a service of deepest mourning. No mass was celebrated and the concentration was on a solemn and penitential commemoration of the Passion. At a certain point a veiled crucifix was brought into the church and when it was unveiled clergy and people crept barefoot and on their knees to kiss the foot of the cross, usually at the sanctuary steps. After the solemn liturgy there was the custom of the burial of Christ in the Easter Sepulchre that had been prepared to the north of the altar. The Host and cross were interred and a watch kept until Easter Sunday when the procession led to the Sepulchre, raised the crucifix and carried it around the church in procession with the bells ringing and the choir singing 'Christus Resurgens'. It was then placed on an altar on the north side of the church and venerated again by the congregation creeping towards it.

It was with the accession of Edward VI that the pace of religious change quickened and St Michael's was affected by the Dissolution of the Chantries Act of 1547. Although there is no actual record of a chantry chapel in St. Michael's it is obvious from the frequent requests for masses for the departed and references to priests to officiate that at least the Chapel of the Blessed Virgin Mary was used for this purpose. The Act was the official disapproval of the doctrine of Purgatory and masses for the dead. No longer was it believed that the prayers of the living could ease the soul's passage through Purgatory before being admitted to heaven All plate and valuables not now needed in the chantries were transferred to the King.

This was followed by the Act of Uniformity 1547. On Whit Sunday 1549 the communion service was heard in English for the first time, becoming the only legally permitted form of worship. For the first time the words were heard which were to resound in St. Michael's for hundreds of years 'THIS DO IN REMEMBRANCE OF ME'. There was further drama because for the first time people in the church were offered the chalice of wine.

It was celebrated in a church unrecognisable by the elderly whose lives had been centred on the Latin Mass and characterised by many outward symbols of their faith.

The main feature of the church had been the great crucifix – the rood – supported on either side by Mary and John. This stood on a wide beam – the rood beam – which carried the main light of the church and which the priest attained by the rood stair in order to read or sing the Gospel. Below the beam was the rood screen on which were painted images of the saints symbolising their dependence on the benefits of Christ's passion. This had filled the arch which marked the separation between nave and the holy chancel. And it was no longer there. It had been cut down.

Within the chancel the stone altar had been the heart of the Catholic faith, the mysterious place where the bread and wine became the body and blood of God. To this shock of physical destruction by hammer blows was added the whitewashing of the wall paintings and the demolition of the

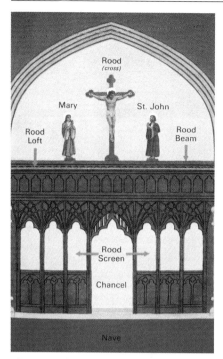

Figure 12. The Rood Screen. Illustration of how the nave and chancel were once separated by the rood screen. (By permission of Lady Bird Books. What to Look For Inside a Church 1972).

saints' statues now known only through the medieval wills. Possibly this was when the statue bases in the chancel and south chapel lost their statues and when the statue bases in the porch were plastered over. Possibly too this was when the monumental brass of John Mew was ripped out.[6] The richly coloured vestments were redundant and the church plate used in ceremonies was no longer required and was confiscated to the Crown. George Whetenhall's zeal would have allowed him to destroy his own family relics in the supposed family Lady Chapel. The aim was to remove all images of the old faith. The medieval 'coloured television' had been switched off. The sound of the chanted mass was heard no more.

At this point the medieval wayside shrines would have been destroyed leaving only the Cross names entrenched in peoples' memories.

The new 'monocrome' channel saw the minister dressed in a permitted long white linen surplice which reached to his feet, standing on the north side of a table placed in the nave with the table ends east and west (not altar wise) In so doing there was no association with the Mass. *'They did not go to the Lord's Board to recreate him again but to feed on him who only once was crucified and offered up. The true use of the Lord's supper was spiritually to eat his body and spiritually drink his blood. Therefore, the form of a table is more suitable for the Lord's board than an altar'.*[7]

With the active support of George Whetenhall whom Becon described as being *'a favourer of the Word'* it can only be supposed that these measures were carried out smoothly. The scene changed on the accession of Queen Mary in 1553 with her determination to restore England to the Roman Catholic faith. She renounced all the changes in religion, the services and appearance of the churches that had been made by Henry VIII and Edward VI during the previous twenty years. Stone altars were to be replaced and the Latin Mass celebrated, chalices and other plate purchased and vestments worn by the priest. Saints days and festivals were returned. It is known that reactions varied to yet another change. Thomas Roydon dictating his will from his new mansion house in 1557 reverts to the old style bequeathing 2s to the vicar of East Peckham for his tithes negligently omitted and gives a suit of vestments of crimson velvet restoring some of the colour so recently lost

But George Whetenhall did not receive the Mass with Thomas Roydon. He was not at St Michael's to witness any Roman Catholic restoration work, nor was he to be found at Hextall Court. He went into exile as a Protestant arriving in Frankfurt in December 1554 with his young son Thomas apparently to avoid Marian persecution. But modern research has shown that this group known as the Marian Exiles who went to Europe did so long before any persecution was thought of and that it was a planned, organised, political migration rather than a flight, directed to the fulfilment of a clearly conceived purpose – that of educating abroad, in an atmosphere unpolluted by idolatry, a body of students of divinity whom it was intended should one day become the clergy of a reformed Anglican Communion. They were men of learning from the two universities of Oxford and Cambridge who went in great numbers aiming to restore religion to its former Protestant state. They lived in communes heavily influenced by John Calvin and in company with the Scottish reformer and preacher John Knox. Their belief in justification by faith and Scripture as the sole rule of faith were at odds with the hierarchical tradition-encrusted rule of Rome. Difficult though was the doctrine which was to cause trouble for many years, that of *'predestination of the elect'*. On return a number of the Marian exiles were the main opponents in Queen Elizabeth's first parliament aiming to prevent her becoming head of the Church of England, rather wishing for open church government without bishops.[8]

But for George Whetenhall and his son Thomas, then aged 20 years, there may have been a suggestion of flight. It is thought that Thomas may have been associated in 1553 with Thomas Wyatt's failed Kentish rebellion to prevent Mary's marriage to the Catholic Philip of Spain. Wyatt, of Allington Castle, who was executed, had also been Thomas' neighbour as lessee of the East Peckham Parsonage. Cuthbert Vaughan, who only avoided execution by informing on other participants, was also a neighbour being the second husband of Elizabeth Roydon, widow of William Twysden of Roydon Hall.

Her monument recording her three husbands is on the south wall of the chapel.

There is no doubt that Hextall Court was a hive of Puritanism, for besides George and Thomas others in the family were involved. On return from exile George's sister Rose married the exile Thomas Wylford of Hartridge, in Cranbrook so enlarging the family circle, Thomas's sister Cecily married another exile, Edwin Sandys, who was later to play a prominent role in the parliamentary opposition to Queen Elizabeth and later still became Archbishop of York. In exile the congregations had become accustomed to a form of Psalm singing in which all present, including women and children, took part. On their return this unusual practice was introduced to their churches in which there had never been any form of congregational singing. Thus the authoritative George may have introduced singing to the ordinary worshippers at St. Michael's!

Certainly the Whetenhalls returned to witness another crisis at St. Michael's. Elizabeth acceded to the throne in 1558 with the determination to

*Figure 13. The Dame Golding Monument. At the top are her paternal arms (*chequy argent gules, a cross azure *Roydon). Below is the motto 'Pietas honoratior annis'. Below this are three shields showing arms of her successive husbands impaling Roydon in each case, Twysden, Vaughan and Golding. At the sides are blank spaces where two shields were originally fixed. Below a lozenge shaped shield defaced.*

restore the religious legislation of her father's later years. This led to another round of church clearance. The hammers were heard again removing the recently reinstalled stone altar and all other items that had been restored during Mary's reign and ensuring that any item that had been overlooked was now removed.

Thus the picture of St. Michael in the stained glass north window of the nave was removed. Fortunately for some reason, someone had scratched on the window.

'HERE STOODE THE WICKED IMAGE OF S. MICHAEL AWAYING OF SOULS BY THE LAWE OF QUENE ELIZABETH ACORDING TO GOD'S HOLY WORD IS TAKEN AWAY.' (weighing)

This inscription was copied by A R Cook in 'A Manor Through Four Centuries', published 1938 but the window was destroyed during the following war. The writing was described by the Rev Bennitt in 1937 as being of the 17th century.

Elizabeth was determined to resolve the confusion of Church Government which had soured the previous years and did so by legislation which gave her the title of Supreme Governor of the Church of England in things ecclesiastical as well as temporal. By another Act of Uniformity 1559 she stamped her authority on every parish in the land;

'All and every person and persons inhabiting within this realm or any other the Queens' Majesty's dominions shall resort to their parish church upon every Sunday and other days ordained and used to be kept as Holy Days and then and there to abide orderly and soberly during the time of Common Prayer, preachings or other service of God there to be used and ministered'.

Again testamentary evidence illustrates the contemporary scene. Apparently attending *'orderly and soberly'* was Robert Downe a wealthy clothier with *'a mansion house and workhouse with all its implements appertaining'* at Beltring. At his death in 1571 he was *'trusting in the merit of Christ's passion that he might be the child of salvation'*.[9]

Unfortunately there were penalties for non attendance and there was the beginning of abuse in the form of persecution of dissidents whether non conforming Protestants or Roman Catholics.

Thus in a short period of twenty years, 1539–59, George Whetenhall saw the beginning of a new age at St. Michael's. He died in 1573 by which time he was grandfather to sons of his own son Thomas who had been in exile with him, so three generations attending the church were influenced by his puritanical views. His character and influence were further reinforced by the fact that he was a highly educated man. After studying at Cambridge he had qualified as a barrister at Gray's Inns of Court and when appointed as Reader reached the height of the legal profession.[10]

Thomas followed his father in the legal profession. Educated at Peterhouse, Cambridge, he also qualified in Law at Gray's Inn and had very firm opinions. Obviously not all people conformed to the new way of thinking and nearing the end of his life he wrote a pamphlet, entitled, *'A Discourse on the Abuses which have Crept into the Churches'*. Dated 1602 *'Anno atatis 74'* (in the seventy fourth year of his age).

One grievance concerned the continual excavation of the church floor for internal burials. This was inconvenient and unsightly for the congregations. The excavation and the construction of a deep vault could mean a long period of disruption while a shallow burial could exude offensive smells. But it was the spiritual aspect which concerned him. He was opposed to burial in church and took drastic action to support his views. He writes:

'This stone like unto a tombstone have I caused here to be laid as a monument in myne own house to signify unto myne posterity that my desire is to be buried honestly and Christianly in the most usual place of burial as in the churchyard of this or another parish where it shall please God to take me unto himself by his mercy obtained through Christ, and not to be buried in any church which is a house of prayer and appointed only to the service of God where God's word ought always on the Lord's day to be preached and man's glory never to be magnified, where the senses ought to be fed with the sacraments and not with painted sepulchres, where the soul ought only to be dedicated unto God and the mind not occupied with any earthly affairs. A house meet for living souls to be assembled and not for dead carcasses to be buried'.[11]

Thus were the community at St. Michael's influenced by such definite beliefs.

His two sons Thomas and Henry followed with similar strong convictions. Raised at Hextal and St. Michael's they also left vivid pictures of church life in those traumatic times by making significant statements of their faith. Although Thomas' statement concerns St. Swithins, his London church, it none the less reflects on his upbringing and the religious thought and language of the period and illustrates the complete break with the old religion. His will, proved 1616, written when he was in the three score and fifth year of his age, weak in body and yet enjoying the faculties of soul and mind stated:

'I do acknowledge and from my heart and soul believe and testify that there is only one true God even the Lord of heaven and earth and of all creation the holy essence of the incomprehensible Trinity, the Father Son and Holy Spirit, three persons and one infinite and all sufficient God the fullness of all perfection, co-eternal, con substantial and individual yet distinguishable as in some measure manifested unto Christ'.

He continues with a further 56 lines of what historians describe as religious ambience but which contain the essence of the change brought about by the break with Rome. Throughout he is convinced that he is one of the predestined Elect. He mounts a vicious attack on the Papists. He abhors the blasphemy of the heretical and idolatrous Papists. He considered that they were more opposite in their opinions to true Christianity than other heretics and more dangerous to true Christianity than Jews or Turks or any other infidels. He abhors the Pope with his idolatrous masses, his pardons and indulgences, his images and his crosses. Writing at the time when Jesuit priests were infiltrating England he ensures that his burial be done *'without gangling of bells, orisons, oblations, priestly processions or other superstitious foolishness'.*

Turning at last to his temporal estate there is the suggestion of family disruption. As his earthly father had settled the estate and lands which came to him by entail from their progenitors chiefly on his younger brother, Sir Henry, and did not leave him anything at all, even though he also provided well for his brothers and sisters, he felt no obligation to leave his own temporal estate to any offspring of his brothers and sisters after the flesh. He appears to have a threefold grudge; not only had his younger brother inherited the estate but he had also received a knighthood, and moreover his father had matched Thomas in marriage in the thirteenth year of his age. He had no wish to malign his brother and seems willing to forgive him because he himself had grievously offended his heavenly father all the days of his life but his attitude to his earthly father seems open to question.

'Although in any matter forgiving my earthly father and my wife to whom by his appointment in the thirteenth year of my age I was matched in marriage I might always wish they lived with the testimony of a good conscience. As David said to Saul "The Lord be judge and plead my cause"'. (This refers to the Biblical story when King Saul had over a long period persecuted David without due cause largely motivated by jealousy of David's success and popularity. David refused to revenge himself for the injustices he had received and left it to God's judgement 1 Samuel 24 v.15.)

He therefore wished to dispose of his temporal estate to the benefit of his spiritual kindred. He was also of the legal profession and a scholarly man with an impressive library containing religious books in Latin, Greek, Hebrew, French, Italian and Spanish. Some he left to family members but the bulk are outlined in another statement in which he establishes a Trust for the benefit of his church St. Swithin's in London. Incidentally his will also opposes his father's view concerning burial!

> *'Thomas Whetenhall eldest son of Thomas Whetenhall whose body lyeth buried under this church having while he lived frequented the ministry of God's word in this place in testimony of his thankfulness to God and of his love of this place, gave in his life time twenty pounds of money towards the enlarging of this church and a high double turning desk of wood and at his own proper cost and charges built this wainscot press and gave the books hereunder named for the use of the minister and lecturer of this place for the time being. And also by his last will and testament he bequeathed £20 of money per annum for the maintaining of a weekly lecture in divinity over and above the lectures hereto usually performed in this place as in the said will more largely may appear. (a copy whereof is in this press)'.*

There follows a catalogue of the books given as a foundation of a bigger library by the above named Thomas Whetenhall esquire. The catalogue contains 56 volumes with Latin titles and two in English being The Acts and Monuments of the Church Commonly Called the Book of Martyrs, two volumes, (published 1597) and Bishop Babbington's Works.[12]

His younger brother, Sir Henry Whetenhall, also of the legal profession, to whom the estate had passed, was knighted when King James I ordered that all men possessed of £40 or more should receive the dignity of knighthood. Dying aged 62 in 1617 the majority of his three page will is also taken up with a statement of his faith but again suggests an undercurrent of future tension in the church.

'In the name of Jesus Christ who died for our transgressions and made his blessed testament that we might receive the promise of eternal inheritance I ordain this my transitory testament and first I commend my soul into the hands of my heavenly Father through Christ my Saviour who in commending his own spirit into his Father's hands did there lay up the safety of the souls of all believers'. He had taken away the partition wall to stop them all out of heaven and had kept the heavenly passage open so that his soul could enter into heaven. In the meanwhile he appointed his body to be committed to the earth safe from the evil works and sorrows of this life being glad to be rid of his afflictions ... at the last day, his body together with his soul would ascend and live for ever with Christ his Saviour.

But *'as the hour of my dissension is only known to God I bow my knees unto him that he grant me in health to wait, in sickness to address myself unto that hour, and in the hour of death that he who is stronger than all will strengthen me against the temptations of Satan, the frailties of nature, the torments of sickness and terrors of death'*.

His children he committed unto God in Christ desiring *'only one thing above all for them that they might be within His covenant seeing that His promises are not made unto us for five or six alone but unto thousands of years beseeching him that all things in their frail pilgrimage in this world work for best unto them and even the miseries of their lives keep them in the narrow way that leads to life eternal'*.

Concerning his temporal estate he opens a window into the domestic life of Hextall Court. He mentions household items, a salt ordinarily used, three white bowls and one great pan and four tongs to be put into the same and one silver basin and ewer, one dozens plain silver spoons, one gilt bowl without a cover and five gilt spoons which belong. Financially he provides for his children, noticeably for Frances so he can continue at university and to follow on to the Inns of Court. Thomas his eldest son and heir to the 'ancient entail' is charged to be kind and careful to his sister Anne and is given responsibility for his loving wife, (the second), *'one that has performed the part of a good mother towards himself and the rest of his brother and sisters'*. But if she *'thinketh not to continue to reside'* with Thomas alternative arrangements are made. In the meanwhile she has the use of the furniture in the best chamber and of the little chamber and all other the featherbed and the stools of her own making as she hath herself made. Sir Henry's fervent prayers for his children were not answered to his desire. Debora married to Robert Multon of St. Cleres died in 1619 aged 22 years, possibly in childbirth leaving a daughter Debora. Frances died young in 1623. Anne did not marry.

It is through his son Thomas, his heir and executor, that the story of the church continues with dramatic consequences.

References

1   A.Cook. A Manor Through Four Centuries 1938.
2   J.F. Thomson. The Later Lollards 1965.
3   Valor Ecclesiasticus. Shoreham Deanery vol I, p144.
4   Calendar Inquisitions Post Mortem Henry VII vol. 3.
5   E Duffy. The Stripping of the Altars 1999.
6   See later Monumental Brasses.
7   E Duffy. op. cit.
8   CH Garret. The Marian Exiles. 1938.
9   There is much evidence of the Wealden weaving industry in neighbouring villages of Yalding and Brenchley researched by Michael Zell. (Industry in the Countryside) However East Peckham was not included in the research because there are no medieval wills and inventories for the Shoreham Deanery. Here however is an East Peckham Clothier who no doubt used the fulling mill at Branbridges. It was an established industry because new fulling mills were built there in 1624. CKS U838 T303.
10 Gray's Inn Administration 1521–1889.
11 LPL MS 445 P314.
12 BL Harlequin Ms No 1500–55 The Achievement of Thomas Whetenhall of East Peckham and the books he left to the church there'. The Harlequin Catalogue is misleading. The document actually refers to Thomas Whetenhall <u>son</u> of Thomas of Whetenhall of East Peckham. He left his books to his London church, not to East Peckham church.

Thomas Whetenhall, Recusant, 1599–1630

Where and how did Thomas with three generations of Puritans influencing him, worshipping in St. Michael's thus with a stronghold of Puritanism engulfing him come to be influenced by the 'heresy' of Roman Catholicism? But the fact is that he became a Roman Catholic, a recusant, (from Latin recuso, I refuse) as did his brother Henry and sister Anne with

Hextal Court now becoming a haven for Roman Catholics. At what point did his stepmother, his father's loving wife notice the difference? What tensions were there in the home and the church? How long did she stay in his home as she saw the evidence of recusancy? Was it reaction to his father's Puritan attitudes that changed his faith?

Considering the terminology of his father's will it is obvious that if Thomas was not already a secret Catholic he was converted soon after his father's death. During Elizabeth's reign Jesuit and seminary priests arrived in England dedicated to the task of restoring Catholicism. As this was seen as disobedience to the Queen the Catholic priests were regarded as traitors. Lay people who were discovered sheltering them could be sentenced to death. By the end of her reign there were known to be three hundred priests working in England and during James reign (1603–1625) seventeen priests were executed. At the parish level those who did not attend church were fined the considerable sum of £20. Thomas' decision as a young man of about 23 years was a bold one because the Catholic population of Kent was very low in comparison to other counties and the strict Protestant stance of the St. Michael's Churchwardens gave him no mercy when obeying the legislation to report recusants to the bishop.

He married Mary Phillips of Fant and by 1623 he is in trouble with the Churchwardens. In their Presentments to the Bishop they describe him as ;

Thomas Whetenhall a papist recusant for failing to have his son baptised within one month of his birth according to the statute.

He was presented again in 1627 for having his son (Thomas) born February 16th 1626 christened privately by, it is conjectured, a seminary priest. (a priest trained overseas). Furthermore it was stated *'that the priests Ward, Wood, and Holland resort to his house and he himself has stood excommunicate since April 26th'*. 'Robert', who was employed by the Whetenhalls as a schoolmaster, was suspected of being a priest.

The same year 1627 other members of the family are indicted, Mary his wife, Henry his brother and Anne his sister together with a group of those, probably estate workers, under his religious protection. Philip Lemion, labourer, Francis Shackerly labourer, Percival Symonds and Jane White spinster are named. In 1629 the unrepentant Whetenhalls were again fined.[10]

His death in 1630 seems unexpected. His will of 1630 has no time for religious preamble. It is briefly, *'I give my soul to God that gave it and my body to be buried in the earth'*. He bequeaths all his lands to his loving wife Mary, appoints executors, Sir Edward Hales his loving cousin, and John Austin, both of Tenterden, refers to legacies in a codicil which does not materialise, acknowledges that he owes his sister Anne gentlewoman of East Peckham, seven hundred pounds, (a huge amount of money which no doubt he had planned to pay back in his life time.) Indeed his time was brief. The will is dated the August 4th and his burial is recorded in the parish register as *'deceased August 5th – entered privately without ye minister'*. It has been thought previously that this refers to the practice of privately burying Papists in the churchyard. These burials sometimes took place in the night with or without the knowledge of the minister when no doubt a Catholic priest conducted an illicit mass for the dead. But it could be that he was a victim of the Bubonic Plague which affected Kent in 1630, although there is no increase of deaths in the register for that year. It is also possible that it was to avoid the considerable expense of a gentleman's funeral, which he could ill afford.

His son Thomas was then a small boy of four years and was only eight years when his mother died in 1634 leaving him as he states in later correspondence *'an orphan at an early age'*.[1] At eleven years of age he would have witnessed a startling change at St. Michael's. It was in 1637 that the policy of Laud, Archbishop of Canterbury, became evident at the church. Laud had for many years opposed Calvinist doctrines and sought to restore something of the pre reformation liturgical practice. He ordered that communion tables should be removed from the nave to the east end of the choir and that they should be railed in to prevent any further movement. This caused hostility from Puritans because it was suggestive of the old altar with its Catholic doctrine of sacrifice and gave that altar more emphasis than the Word preached from the pulpit. In St. Michael's the pulpit was a sensitive feature for the vicar. Mr.Worral records in the parish register that *'In the same year also was a new pulpit given to the church by Mr. Thomas Twysden Esq. and Councillor at law who gave the same at his own proper costs and charges. Francis Worral then vicar hath registered the memory of the same to succeeding ages'*.

Another witness to the railing in of the altar was Sir Roger Twysden who described the scene, *'as we now see it'*. He wrote that the communion table was removed to the top of the chancel and placed in the old position, altar wise, (ends north and south) with rails about the table. Seats of wainscot were made against the wall for communicants' use. A further description enhances the scene in that *'the communion table is close to the wall'* and that *'the new wainscot on the east side of the table is made with pictures of angels therein carved'*. This suggested popery as did the even more telling complaint that the Vicar, Mr. Worral refused to administer the Sacrament of the Lord's Supper to one of the inhabitants of the said parish, *'although in decent manner he did desire the same, and offered himself in the Chancel and all because the said inhabitant would not come up to the rail to receive the same'* because this was suggestive of Popery. The church was so dissatisfied with Mr. Worral that they complained to Parliament in 1640 *'that he was also vicar of Wateringbury and doth many times serve the Cure himselfe of both these parishes and is soe uncertayne in officiating his cure that, our parish being spacious, the parishioners cannot come to church with any convenience in the morning, and at other times (at time accustomed in other parishes) loste their labour, he being dispatcht and gone to his cure in Wateringbury. He is very negligent in preaching, insomuch that we have not a Sermon at our Parish above once a fortnight. (except it be a funerale Sermon which is very seldom.)'*.[2] Evidence of at least one funeral sermon comes from the will of William Baker 1619 who bequeathed 10s to Mr. Worral to preach a sermon at his funeral. Perhaps it is ironic that his own funeral with a sermon is recorded in St. Michael's register:

> *'1652 Francis Worral once vicar of this parish was buried in the church porch of Wateringbury on the 24th of May and here registered for memorial by me William Polly now vicar in present who buried him and preached at his funeral.'*

It is this small boy Thomas Whetenhall whose very baptism in 1627 was so dramatic who leaves his mark on the later story of St. Michael's. He grew up in the troublesome times leading to the Civil War and Commonwealth which were to have great effect on the church and people.

References
1   BL Ms 4713 Thomas Whetenhall letter to his cousin John Gibbon 1677.
2   Lambert Larkin. Proceedings Principally in the County of Kent. Camden Society lxxx, 1861. Available in CKS library.

3. The Commonwealth Parish

The social, religious and political disagreements between King Charles I and Parliament erupted into the Civil War, the defeat of the King and the establishment of the Commonwealth. The effects of this on the church were immense. All previous ecclesiastical Acts of Elizabeth's reign were repealed and made void. This repeal included the use of the Prayer book which was replaced by a Directory for Public Worship. A new Act was introduced:

> 'all and every persons within this Commonwealth shall (having no reasonable excuse for their absence) upon every Lord's day, days of public thanksgiving and humiliation, diligently resort to some public place where the service and worship of God is exercised'. Those not in accordance would be taken as offenders against the law 'and shall be proceeded against accordingly'.

Church wardens were told to present recusants of any belief, those who did not conform, to the Bishop and Justices of the Peace. They were told to disarm in particular all papist recusants of their weapons. Papists were defined as those who had not gone to church more than once in a month or who had two or more recusant servants.

Of the 450 benefices in Kent 233 Anglican clergy refused to take the oath now required:

> 'I do declare and promise that I will be true and faithful for the Commonwealth of England as it is now established without a king or House of Lords'.

They were ejected from their livings and endured much hardship, many being imprisoned, while the income from their livings were given to Puritan ministers. Mr. Worral, of previous complaint, having been vicar for twenty seven years was ejected from the parish and his home in 1644 and replaced by the Puritan minister John Topping. The new minister gave satisfaction not only to East Peckham but to the Puritans of Brenchley who had frequently complained that their minister Mr. Gilbert refused to baptise their children according to the New Directory. As a result 'divers infants remained unbaptised some of them being about a year old'. They ordered therefore 'that ye parents of such children do bring them unto ye parish church at East Peckham where we do desire that Mr. Topping would baptise them according to the said Directory'.[1]

Within the church Laud's railed communion table was moved from the chancel into the nave where the congregation could once again gather round to remove any suggestion of Romish practice.

Missing from his place at the communion table was Sir Roger Twysden of Roydon Hall for he himself was a prisoner of conscience. In the events leading to the Civil War he would not allow himself to side either with King or Parliament. His only loyalty was to the law of England. He was accused by Parliament of being one of the chief organisers of the famous Petition of Kent drawn up by the gentry of Kent and presented to Parliament. Of the seventeen points presented in the Petition some were religious and particularly offensive to the Puritan dominated House. These points defended the Common Prayer Book and the appointment of traditional Bishops to administer the church. Both of these features Parliament intended to remove. Others were of a practical political nature but famously the observation of a basic principle was demanded:

'that the precious liberty of the subject, the common birthright of every English man may be as in all other points preserved entire so in this also, that no order of either or both houses not grounded on the laws of the land may be enforced on the subject, until it be fully enacted by Parliament'.[2]

Figure 14. Sir Roger Twysden. The original hangs in Bradbourne House East Malling. (By permission of the Kent Archaeological Society.)

It was ironic that Sir Roger should be treated so unlawfully in the following years. He was never charged with an offence because there was no law he had offended.

He was arrested in March 1642 at Roydon Hall by order of the House of Commons and imprisoned in London. Although he was bailed for £5000 and his own £10,000 and released he was ordered not to go into Kent.

His absence had an immediate effect on the parish especially concerning the relief of the poor as described by the Churchwardens and Overseers of the Poor who wrote to him that same year in London. They said that in consequence of the heavy increase of the poor in these troublesome times *'they humbly craved him to continue his yearly contribution as formerly he had been assessed and so much the rather because the charge is greater in regard there is nobody inhabiting Mr. Whetenhall's house'.* They beseeched him to send a word or two in writing so that they could proceed accordingly to relieve the poor. His long term absence and his inability to pay owing to the loss of his income must have had a profound effect on the parish.[3]

His homesickness and shock is apparent in his letter to his wife:

'I enquire of you what state the deer are and wonder much that they are so backward, they thriving most in such weather. I thank thee for thy sugar cakes my dear heart which will be very useful to me. Farewell again and again my own dear heart whom I never knew to be parted from till now'.

Although he was allowed home in May he was arrested again in August and confined to an inn, The Three Tobacco Pipes, near Charing Cross. So distressed was he at his treatment that he recorded events and his thoughts for his family in order that they might learn and avoid a repetition in the future. These manuscripts, now in the British Library, were not intended for publication but two hundred years later they were published as his 'Journal'.[4]

He recorded the outrage of torture committed by Parliamentarian soldiers at Barham Court, Teston. The rumour that Roydon Hall would be attacked the next night led his wife to disperse the family and *'although exceeding weak not having recovered from her lying in, full of fright and fear came up to London on horseback ... my wife weak and sick as she was retired to her house in London, my family dispersed, myself in prison, out of mind'.* His London home was searched and Roydon Hall was raided at night by thirty troopers searching for evidence of arms and other warlike provision but they found none. In despair he attempted to escape to France but his failure and capture led to his imprisonment in a disreputable prison The Counter at Southwark.

Soon came the greatest indignity. His estate was sequestered and its income taken by Parliament. He was deprived not only of its income and of its management but of its future for the famous Roydon oaks, one important source of his income, were cut down. He wrote that he stood seeing his little estate wither away yet had no power of helping it. There was no money for the expenses of his imprisonment, for the support of his wife, five children and his servants. Eventually after great persistence, travelling many miles to attend committee meetings where she was treated insolently, Isabella, his wife was granted a small portion of the rents.

Throughout the years of detention and humiliation by his tormentors he refused to compromise. He maintained that he was innocent. He described his treatment as monstrous. Eventually he was offered terms by which he could regain his estate, by in fact, admitting that he had done wrong, but those terms were entirely against his principles. He was still demanding to know the charge against him when his brother in law, so distressed at the destruction at Roydon, persuaded him to accept a pitifully small financial settlement, although he was still sequestered.

It was in August 1647 that he came home to East Peckham. Dame Isabella records in her diary, *'My husband came to Peckham where he had not been in five years before having been a prisoner most of that time by Parliament'.* But unjust financial demands by Parliament continued and Roydon Hall was again searched for arms in 1651. Dame Isabella records the frightening experience when *'at four o'clock in the morning came troopers to our house at Peckham to search, as they said, for arms and letters, for letters there were none they cared for, yet carried away 4 or 5 of my husband's and arms and carried away my husband and brother Cholmley prisoner to Leeds Castle but no charge could be made against him'.*[5]

Sir Roger ends his journal saying that he has shown how he fell into these troubles and how God in his good time in part delivered him out of them. There remained *'that I render him all humble and hearty thanks for his gracious assistance to me and mine during the continuance of them and in the end by an unexpected hand freeing this nation of their heavy taskmasters, that men may live quietly and enjoy with more freedom their own houses and thoughts'.*

Sir Roger Twysden belongs to St. Michael's. He is famous for his historical manuscripts, many researched and written whilst imprisoned and now conserved and consulted by scholars world wide in the British Library.[6] He is famous for the part he played in the Civil War and Commonwealth years. He is famous for his character as an English gentleman, land owner and family man, but his heart was at Roydon Hall, his home and his church. Recording the death of his wife he writes that she is buried *'in our little burying place in East Peckham church'.* *'With what patience she for my sake endured that loathsomeness of a most nasty prison called the Counter in Southwark, that she might have my company only. With what wisdom she solicited then and afterwards my business at committees and at the House of Commons sometimes itself. With what magnanimity she went through those miserable times I shall not here write because I have not words to express it'.*

Typically he made arrangements for his own funeral. Writing in his will he reflects that, *'It is fit for every man in his youth and greatest strength to remember his creator and prepare himself for his last home, much more for me who has lived to the age of 72 years ... I therefore Roger Twysden well in body and mind do now make my will and testament that I may not have it to do nor disturb my thoughts when it shall please my God and Saviour Jesus Christ, God and Man, to call me unto him into whose hands and protection I commit my soul'.* After his personal bequests he wishes; *'As for my burial I will it be in the parish church of East Peckham by my ancestors and there to lay me as nigh my wife as may be that we may rise together when God shall call us – and I will that my funeral be with as little charge as is possible and therefore my burial be without invitation of any neighbours. I would have a stone with an inscription, that which I would have written on it my son will find in one of my books of accounts either the beginning or at the end'.*[7]

That stone erected 1689 remains in the church. It was inscribed in classical Latin and therefore for 315 years it has been unreadable for the majority of people. The translation by Geoffrey Allibone is believed to be the first. It is there that Sir Roger finds words to express his wife's magnanimity for posterity. The translation can be seen on page 87.

By arranging for his son to record his genealogy he had repeated a family tradition. Roger's own father William, here recorded, had erected his own parents' monument to be seen on the south wall of the chapel. It records that an earlier Roger Twysden and his wife Ann *'though they were born on the same day yet died they severally'*, Anne 1592 aged 50 and Roger 1603 age 61. Thus they had lived through the disruptive years of the Reformation church and testified that *'They lived in the faith and love of our Lord Jesus and died in Hope. In their lives were blest of God and beloved of men'.* Of their twelve children six were deceased. *'His son erected this monument to them all 1611'.*

Dying in 1672 Sir Roger had previously mourned his sister Elizabeth, wife of Sir Hugh Cholmley who had been a fellow sufferer in the Civil War. Hugh had first fought for the Parliamentarians but changed his allegiance to the King and defended Scarborough Castle for a long period before being forced to surrender in 1645. Throughout the long siege Elizabeth endured the hardships with him, and also nursed the wounded and sick. When her husband was forced by Parliament to live on the continent she remained striving to restore the family estate in Whitby, Yorkshire and was separated from him for five years. She returned to her home at Roydon whenever she could and it was here that she requested to be buried in the Twysden aisle of St. Michael's church rather than in Whitby. She was joined by her husband whose epitaph is added to hers:

'Here also is buried the body of Sir Hugh Cholmley her husband who for the great love he bore the virtue and worth he found in the said Elizabeth declined the being interred in his county among his ancestors and chose to be laid beside her by whom he had six children'. The Cholmley Coat of Arms make a vivid display in the corner of the chapel.

On the chancel wall is the epitaph to Thomasin Wareham who lived for fifty two years in the families of Sir Roger and Sir William sharing their faith and worshipping in this church. *'She died in the 70th year of her age in 1688 generally loved and esteemed'.* When Dame Isabella was asking excuse from abstinence from meat in Lent in 1640 *'Thomasin their gentlewoman being of a sick and weak constitution'* was also excused.[8]

Sir Roger lived to see the restoration of the King to the throne in 1660. The occasion is recorded in the parish register:

'John, son of Stephen Cheesman and Barbara, daughter of Thomas Cheesman were baptised in the 12th year of the reign of Sovereign Lord Charles ye second by me William Pollhill'.

The years of the Commonwealth were over. It was indeed the 12th year of the King's reign for his accession is dated from the date of his father's execution in 1649.

In the church the communion table was again moved – this time from the nave back to the east end of the chancel where it was railed in and was once again referred to as the altar. The Puritan Directory was disowned and the Prayer Book reintroduced in 1662 with some alterations. Unfortunately, for some, no effort was made to restore the tippling house outside the church which Anthony Weldon, the detested Chairman of the Puritan County Committee had caused to be pulled down because '*it gave disturbance by noise and tippling in the time of church service*'![6]

The puritan minister Mr. Polly, was replaced in the vicarage by Mr. Samuel Grimes. The latter had previously been appointed vicar of Hadlow in 1628 but about 1645 he had been ejected by Parliament on account of his royalist sympathies.[7] It seems most likely that he had been involved with his brother John, Vicar of Igtham in the famous local event recorded by Rushworth, the historian of his day.[8]

It appears that John Grimes refused either to take the Vow or Covenant or to read it out to his parishioners as he was required to do by order of both Houses. '*Therefore a party of horse was sent to take him up to Parliament but several persons in that town and the places adjacent gathered together with halberts, swords and staves and would have rescued him which though they could not effect yet, being up in tumult many others resorted to them and at the town of Sevenoaks they increased their number almost to 2,000.*' The Parliament sent down Sir Henry Vane in order to appease them offering them protection if only they would return to their houses. This was refused and Colonel Richard Brown was sent with two regiments of foot and a regiment of dragoons and some troops of horse who drove them from Sevenoaks to Tonbridge where a party of them '*having pulled down Hildenbridge about a quarter of a mile from the town did from the hill beyond it, make a stiff opposition for some time*'. Concerning John it is not surprising that the report concludes, '*He was expelled by Parliament*'.

It is possible that Samuel was imprisoned. Certainly his personal estate in Hadlow was sequestered by Parliament leaving his wife without an income. For over a year she had to plead to the Committee for Plundered Ministers for the payment of an income until Parliament allowed her one fifth of the rents.[9] He had been restored in 1660 when he signed the loyal address of Kent Ministers and was appointed to East Peckham in 1661 after sixteen years of deprivation. His Probate Inventory shows that he had been living very comfortably in the spacious vicarage with four hearths and 11 rooms, including a bay containing 'the school' with its separate parlour, kitchen and school chamber, and another bay with a range of domestic rooms comprising brew house, milk house, cheese house, butteries and kitchen. The evidence of comfort is found in his parlour which contained a carpet, six cushions and window curtains as well as furniture. The total of his inventory was £160 of which the greatest item was £15 for the books in his study.[10]

Unfortunately he had not enjoyed his peace for long because his will is dated June 10 1664 and the inventory was taken a short time after. He states that he is weak in body but of sound and perfect memory and is leaving his soul '*in the hands of Almighty God in the name of the passion of Christ Jesus my only Lord and only Saviour*'. For this cause he had suffered much as had his neighbours Sir Roger Twysden and Thomas Whetenhall (see later).

His successor Richard Marsh was to have a quieter life for 25 years dying in 1679 asking to be buried in the church porch of East Peckham decently and privately. He lies inside the west porch where the indent of his brass inscription still remains.

References

1 Lambert Larkin op cit.
2 Elizabeth Melling. Kentish Sources. Kent and the Civil War.
3 CKS. Lambert Larking Papers.
4 AC vols 1-4 the Journal of Sir Roger Twysden 1859–62.
5 AC v51 The Diary of Isabella wife of Sir Roger Twysden. 1939.
6 CKS U1823/2 F6.
7 Walker. Sufferings of the Clergy.
8 Rushworth. vol 3.
9 BL 15670 Minute Books of the Committee for Plundered Ministers.
10 PCC Prob4/ 18238 Inventory of Samuel Grimes.

The Hearth Tax, Village and Church

The Hearth Tax, introduced in 1662, was a major source of government revenue being based on the number of hearths in a house. Each householder, excepting those on poor relief or living in a house worth less than £1 a year, was obliged to pay 2s a year for every hearth. The list of East Peckham householders, as given on Lady Day 1664 with their names and the number of hearths in their home gives some idea of their status. As it includes those unable to pay, it is a complete picture of the village households in that year showing 134 houses in which an estimated 500 people lived all of whom were required by law to attend the parish church.[1] Even allowing for human exigencies a congregation of several hundred can be assumed to have assembled in St. Michael's church on Sundays. Possibly missing were *'those such as do abuse the Sabbath day as swearing, drunkenness and other such abuse'* duly reported by the churchwardens to the Bishop in 1670.

For administration purposes the tax was collected in the three ancient boroughs of the parish – Upper Borough and Loneborough in the north in Littlefield Hundred and the larger Stockenbury to the south in Twyford Hundred.

Upper Borough

Sir Roger Twysden . .30	Mr. Samuel Grimes . .4	Mr.Ralph Lowe 2	Thomas Sumers 6
John Parkinson 3	Henry Godfrey 1	Robert Arnol 1	Anthony Hickmott . .4
Walter Brooke 4	George Sedgewick . . .3	Widow Smyth 1	Robert Milles 3
Martin Startup 3	James Hunt 1	Arthur Cheesman . .1	John Johnson 1
Josias Bell 2			

Not Chargeable

John Jervis 2	Stephen Walter 1	Elizxabeth Bates . . .1	Widdow Wodgate . . .1

Lone Borough

Sir Humphrey Miller* 4	Thomas Whetnall Esq .13	Edward Manlcy gcnt . 6	Richard Summers . . .4
James Hayes 1	John Knell 1		

Not Chargeable

Thomas Somners 1	Widdow Luck 1

Borough of Stockenbury

John Stanford 2	Thomas Bishop 2	Thomas Dann 2	John Cheesman jun . .2
Richard Bennet 2	Thomas Cheesman . .1	Widow Martin 1	John Cheesman sen . .2
William Huggens 2	William Coe 2	Widdow Cockrell . .2	Widdow Stone 2
Henry Huggens 1	Thomas Jewell 1	James Freeman 2	Henry Wakelin 2
Thomas Field 1	Richard Hilles 1	John Stone 2	Peter Beecher 1
William Freeman 1	Bartholomew Hodge .1	John Johnson 1	John Butler 3
John Biggenden 2	John Finch 1	William Day 1	Thomas Paulie 1
William Dennis 1	Stephen Allen 1	Widdow Biggenden 1	John Checksfield 2
John Symmons 2	George Pattenden . . .2	Richard Freeman . .1	William Pattenden . . .1
Widdow Thompson . .1	James Freeman 1	John Judd 2	Widdow Marten 2
Thomas Best 1	Iden Plane 2	William Rofe 2	Francis Plane 1
Richard Stanford 2	John Keeble 2	Isaiah Symmons** .3	Widdow Turke 2

Henry Standford	2	Thomas Bennet	1	John Barnes	2	Thomas Hatch	2
James Gardiner	1	Marten Gibbons	1	Thomas Symmons	.2	Richard Hatch	1
Michael Cheesman	..1	Robert Sadell	2	Robert Browne	1	Henry Cheesman**	..3

Not Chargeable

Thomas Smyth	2	John Head	1	John Dennis	1	Widow Honey	1
Mary Spirke	1	Thomas Medhurst	...1	Robert Burr	1	William Luck	1
William Allingham	..1	Nicholas Barefoot	...1	John Day	1	John Parker	1
William Sparke	1	John Crowhurst	1	Widow King	1	John Willard	1
Thomas Luck	1	Thomas King	1	John Webb	1	Widdow Frummons	..1
William Shaw	1	Richard Cheeseman	..2	John Smyth	1	George Luck	1
Francis King	1	Thomas Stanford	1	John Children Sen	.1	John Children jun	...1
Huggin Plane	1	Widdow Tebb	1	John Best	1	Elizabeth Barefoot	...1
Richard Willard	1	Widdow Butcher	1	John Lilley	1	Stephen Cheeseman	.1
Christopher Gardiner	.1	William Waller	1	John Gibbons	1	Widdow Baker	1
Reynold Evans	1	John Jewell	1				

* In an empty house.

** In two houses.

Research has revealed where some of these people lived. Their various occupations give a glimpse into their society. Josias Bell was a glover living at Bell's Farm; Thomas Dann, a yeoman at Burrs Oak; Iden Plane, a Maltster on the Cates Court site on Hale Street; John Barnes at what is now the Rose and Crown; William Rolfe, blacksmith on the corner of Hale Street and Smithers Lane; Stephen Cheeseman at 23 Smithers Lane; Widdow Biggenden at Two Ashes, Bush Lane; Richard Stanford at what is now called The Nursing Home in Old Road; John Butler, miller at Little Mill and John Cheksfield was a victualler at the Bull House, Snoll Hatch, now called Well Cottage. Sources also reveal that James Hunt was a blacksmith, James Gardiner a bricklayer, Richard Wakelyn a cordwainer and Richard Willard a Cooper.[2]

Richard Hatch at Goodwins Farm now known as Old Well Cottage on Hale Street represents the Commonwealth 'man in the street'. He had no claim to fame. Although married and buried at the church he is one of the thousands who have no monument there among the famous but like them he lived through the uncertainties of the civil war period. In February 1660 he married Anne Cheesman at St. Michael's and on March 31st needing a home for his bride he took the lease of Goodwin's Farm, Hale Street, with its 42 acres. Richard agreed that Mrs. Solomon, a widow, who was leasing the farm, could hang out her washing and walk in the gardens until mid summer's day June 21 but in the meantime she had to come to a lot of arrangements with Richard because the house was by then about two hundred years old and was badly in need of repair. In fact it seems ruinous – it needed a new roof – new walls – a new floor in the hall and milk house and it needed new boards to floor the chamber over the parlour. As well as agreeing to supply seasoned wood to floor the chamber over the parlour and the nails, loam, lime and sand needed for the repairs Mrs. Solomon agreed to put a sink in the new kitchen and a well of water *'with steppes for taking and dipping of water near to the said kitchen'*. Richard agreed to take up the old floor boards and use them to repair the barn because that was also in need of repair as was the malt house and the wheat chamber.[3] His later probate inventory shows that he modernised the house by changing the design from the old custom of sleeping downstairs in the parlour to moving the sleeping arrangements upstairs. It was no doubt in their 'best chamber' the room over the parlour, newly floored by Richard, containing the listed feather bed with its bolster and pillows, blankets and coverlettes, that shielded by its curtains Anne gave birth to their child nine years later. Hopefully Richard was in the comfort of that bed when he died unexpectedly that same year, 1669 without making a will. His wife was left to cope with her baby and the farm and the problems of intestacy the legalities of which took two years before the probate inventory was completed.[4]

Over all it was a community which had settled down after the civil unrest of the past. It appears to have been a young community with marriages at St. Michael's increasing dramatically between 1650 and 1660 to about three times the level experienced both before and after this period.[5]

Of the 29 houses in the northern area 14 were of high quality while 15 had one or two hearths. In marked contrast, in the southern area, of the 105 houses 70 had one hearth and 33 had 2 and only one person had 3 (the 43 exempt were mostly single hearths). Thus it would appear that the majority of houses were small, timber framed, hall houses not yet upgraded to 'modern' heating with new brick stacks replacing plaster chimneys and heating new rooms over the hall. This may be due to the constraints of the main landlords, Sir Roger Twysden and Thomas Whetenhall, both of whom had suffered financially during the troubled years of religious and civil unrest, Sir Roger with the loss of his famous oaks and Thomas' payments of considerable recusancy fines.

Although the Hearth Tax is a Parliamentary record it also serves as a record of those who had come through a turbulent period of history, during which battles both civil and spiritual had been fought and the results accepted. Perhaps the spiritual battle is summed up in the 1666 will of Arthur Cheesman of Snoll Hatch who declares that *'I do die in the true and ancient faith of the Church of England'*.[6]

References

1 For a detailed study of the East Peckham Hearth Tax see Harrington,Pearson and Rose. The Kent Hearth Tax Assessment Lady Day 1665, pages lxxvii -xiii. Published British Record Society and Kent Archaeological Society, 2000.
2 CKS Shoreham Deanery Wills and Inventories.
3 CKS U48 T18 Lease to Richard Hatch.
4 CKS SD Inventories.
5 D. Maynard East Peckham Parish Registers. Computerised. See 'Trends' in Miscellaneous Items.
6 CKS SD Wills Arthur Cheesman 1666.

Thomas Whetenhall Recusant 1626–1704

However not all were within the Church of England. Thomas, whose very baptism had been dramatic, upheld his Catholic faith throughout the further dramatic events of his life. His brother George born 1623, according to the Presentments, was also a Papist recusant but died intestate at eighteen years in 1641 leaving young Thomas unexpectedly the heir to the estate. According to the Probate Administration a guardian was appointed during his minority.[1] He was to be an early victim of the media. He became the husband of Elizabeth Bedingfield who was married to him at the age of 16 years and whose tomb lies in the church near the chancel arch. She is remembered by her family, the Bedingfelds of Oxburgh Hall Norfolk as *'La Blanche Whetenhall'* and the portrait clearly illustrating her beauty hangs in the private wing at Oxburgh. Although her beauty is undisputed her description by Anthony Hamilton in the Memoirs of Le Comte de Gramont is thought to have undertones of malice. He describes her as an *'essential English beauty, her colouring was a composite of lilies and roses, snow and milk, her arms and hands, her bosom and her feet were so delicate that they might have been modelled out of wax: her features were of the finest and most charming'*. Thomas on

Figure 15. Elizabeth Whetenhall, second wife of Thomas Whetenhall. The original painting hangs in the private wing of Oxburgh Hall, Norfolk. (By permission of the National Trust.) Author's photograph.

the contrary is described as being a much older man who had been studying for the church until his brother died and he took over the inheritance of the estate. But after his marriage he continued to pore over his books, went to bed early in order to get up early to study with the result that his wife had no companionship with him and no conversation either because she did not understand his theology. Hamilton writes that it was natural that she found East Peckham extremely boring with her elderly husband paying more attention to his books than to her youthful charms. Literary opinion is that Hammond was wickedly malicious and the dating of the incidents in his narrative are inaccurate.[2]

In fact, Thomas was a mere 29 years in 1655 when he married Elizabeth and as to his portrayal as an elderly, boring man nothing could be further from the truth as another writer has recorded concerning his earlier life.

It is true that he did study for the church, entering the English College at Rome at the age of 19 years under the name of Stanley, but he did not continue. It was while Thomas was in Europe that he met Catherine Talbot second daughter of the banished Earl of Shrewsbury. The Shrewsbury family were one of the most powerful families in England before the Civil War and confidants to the throne. Catherine's chaperon Richard Lascelles was later to make:

'*A relation of her voyage from Brussels into Italy for to serve her afterwards in England to put her in mind of those things which she had seen in her journey*'. This is now preserved in the British Library as '*The Voyage of Lady Catherine Whetenhall dedicated to his most noble friend Thomas Whetenhall Esq*'.[3] Thus Lascelles came unexpectedly to record a romance and tragedy of great poignancy. Writing to Thomas after the sad events he had recorded he explains how he was '*an eyewitness from the first birth and upward of the singular affection you mutually bore one another*'. He recalls how Thomas dispatched from Brussels to obtain her father's consent for the marriage and with what impatience, that being obtained, he suffered the '*dilatory treaties of portions and settlements and how finally with passion he broke all delays posting over into Flanders and entrusting the final conclusions of business into the hands of friends who had orders to satisfy anything rather than any further procrastination. He was covetous of nothing in the world but her person and for it he would at all time forfeit not only a part but the whole of his estate*'.

The time of waiting ended when her ladyship returned from Brussels to Louvain where on September 1st 1649 she was married to Thomas Whetenhall esq. in the church of the English Nuns '*to the great contentment of them both and the satisfaction of their friends.*' It was said that their souls were so sympathetic that whatever the music or the book they were as one.

After the wedding however her ladyship expressed her desire of undertaking the Holy Pilgrimage to Rome. His willingness to agree to her request was evident but there was conflict in his mind as to the fears and dangers that might attend so great a challenge.

His fears were to be realized because having arrived in the famous university and tourist town of Padua in Italy her Ladyship fell sick and was confined to bed but *'not for one moment did her young husband leave her, neither night nor day for a whole month, not even after the child was brought to birth'*. Hundreds of masses were sung for her but after all the moving details of the death bed scene described by Lascells she submitted to the inevitable on July 6th.

It was left to Thomas to arrange a funeral just ten months after a wedding. She was buried in the Oratorium Church of Padua dedicated to St. Thomas of Canterbury. *'He caused a great vault to be made in the midst of the church covered with a tombstone and epitaph with a long mortuary cloth of black blazoned with a white cross.'*.

The epitaph was dedicated:

'To the beloved and eternal memory of a wife beyond deserts' and records the biographical details that she was the daughter of the venerable English blood of the house of Talbot, John, Earl of Shrewsbury.

Loving even in death her husband Thomas Whetenhall deposited her here.
She died the day before the Nones of July 1650
In expectation of her virtue flowering into eternal life
Her life was a flower of virtue for the Reaper.[4]

'It was a pious and moving sight to see that sad husband kneeling at Mass before her hearse with twenty poor beggars to whom he gave alms for thirty days after they had prayed with him'. A thousand masses were sung for her and the whole town of Padua showed their feelings for the loss of his love by writing epitaphs and eulogies.

This was not the end of the story. After the death Richard Lascels *'delivered to Thomas every item which had been her Ladyships'* because every little book and paper which had been hers Thomas held in great esteem. It appears that he held her in such esteem that he brought her home with him for during the Victorian church restoration in 1856 carpenters who were installing new pews in the church dug up an old casket containing a perfect heart. The report in the Kentish Gazette supposed that it belonged to one of

Figure 16. Tomb of Elizabeth Whetenhall, second wife of Thomas Whetenhall. © Colin Rainer.

Figure 17. Tomb of Catherine Whetenhall, 'third wife of the thrice unfortunate Thomas'. © Colin Rainer.

the Whetenhall family because it was found under their pew where the Whetenhalls used to sit.[5]

At the time of her death in 1650 he was but 24 years old. It was not until five years later, still only 29 years old, that he married the 16-year-old Elizabeth Bedingfield of Paston in Norfolk and was 40 years in 1664 when she died at the age of 28. Of Elizabeth he records on her tombstone near the chancel arch that *'She faithfully and exemplarily discharged the part of an affectionate wife, dutiful child, and sincere friend and which comprehends all of a good Christian. Her death left a general sadness but with her husband so great a resentment as he could rather wish engrave his own than her monument'.*

This is not the old boring man wrongly described by The Comte de Gramont. Another example of his affectionate nature speaks from the epitaph of Elizabeth Whetenhall's grandfather Edward Paston who is buried beside her.

> *'Here lieth Edward Paston of Beckhall in Norfolk who transported thence with affection to his grand children Thomas and Elizabeth Whetenhall Put here a period to this life's travailles leaving himself as a pledge of his love to them whilst they to him return this sad monument of their resentment.*
> *Feb 1654/55 aetat 63 Requiescat in pace.'*

As yet Thomas, twice bereaved, had no family but at 42 years old in 1666 he married Anne Anglesye daughter of Francis Saunders of Shankton in Leicestershire and Dame Catherine Jerningham of Cossey in Norfolk. Her story is recorded on her tombstone dated 1689.

Thomas refers to her as *'the third wife of the thrice unfortunate Thomas (now 63 years) who after a pious charitable and most exemplary life finished her happy course in the one and fiftieth year of her age after three and twenty years of marriage'* but she left behind *'four disconsolate children Henry, Thomas, Catherine and Elizabeth'.* His two daughters bearing the names of his previous two wives.

She lies displaying the arms of the Whetenhall family, impaled with that of Saunders of Leicestershire charged with elephants. Attached to a helmet is the Whetenhall crest – a goat's head 'erased'. There is no indication of the trials she had endured, for the Whetenhall troubles had continued as recorded in the Calendar of Assize records[5].

Thomas Whetenhall was reported for keeping a priest at his house, Thomas Fowler in 1670 and James Pritchard in 1671. In 1675 a list of recusants *'who have not received communion these ten years passed'* seems like a roll call of those who have kept their Roman faith; Thomas Whetenhall and Anglisia his wife, George Baker servant, John Parkinson and his wife, William Weller and his wife, Henry Godfrey and his wife, Richard Bennet's widow.[6]

Their position in the parish is shown in the Compton census ordered by Bishop Compton of London in 1676 to survey the strength of Catholicism and dissent in England and Wales.[6]

The entry for East Peckham in the Shoreham Deanery reports that:

> *There are inhabiting within the parish of East Peckham 350 persons above the age of 16 years. There are resident amongst these inhabitants professed Papist recusants.*
> *Thomas Whetenhall and Anglissa his wife.*
> *George Baker Dorothy Rogers*
> *Eliza Parkinson and Eliza Goodwin his servants*
> *John Parkinson and his wife, William Brumminger.*
> *Henry Godfrey Senior and his wife.*
> *Henry Waller and his wife.*

In Mereworth which had a smaller population of 170 there were 10 Papists; in Tonbridge there were 12 but none in the surrounding villages. In the whole Rochester Deanery of 99 towns and villages there remained only 64 Roman Catholics. This illustrates the singular nature of the Roman Catholic stronghold of 14 in East Peckham supported by the Whetenhall household.

Thomas continued to be persecuted; in 1680 for travelling more than five miles from his normal place of abode (The Five Mile Act) and on several subsequent occasions, and in 1686 for retaining recusant servants in his house for three months in addition to the 'normal' recusant charges.

He was banned from taking part in County affairs as had been family custom, unable to attend university and so enter the legal profession as had been the family tradition.

Yet it was a burden that Thomas carried willingly. He was distantly related to Sir Roger Twysden. As an older man of some 62 years Twysden was corresponding in 1659 with the younger Thomas showing great concern for what he considered was his misguided faith. The letters reveal that the two had spent much time in Sir Roger's closet at Roydon where there was access to his books. They discussed the canon of scripture, papal supremacy, transubstantiation and referred constantly to the writings of the early Church Fathers. But neither was willing to give in to the others view. Sir Roger, convinced that he is right, urgently advises, 'Consider dear sir, it is no less than your own soul is the price at stake'. To which Thomas had his answer, 'The Church is my security and in a grateful return of that happy tranquillity which I experience by relying on her.' None the less the friendship was genuine. Sir Roger was familiar with his birth and family tragedies and assures Thomas that his letters came 'from one who truly loves you.[7] Roger Twysden invited Thomas, who after all was a relative, to his daughter's wedding.

Also reported by the Churchwardens to the Bishop had been Anabaptists, William Day, William Huggins, Robert Godfrey and his wife in 1668. Stephen Allan and John Day were excommunicated in 1668 and again in 1676.

On the Compton Census they are termed as 'other dissenters who obstinately refuse and wholly absent themselves from the communion of the Church of England' and presumed to be Anabaptists because William Huggins, William Day, Robert Godfrey and his wife head the list. New names, John Terry and his wife, George Martin, Richard Bennet and William Browning may indicate an ongoing cause. The Anabaptists, who refused to baptise infant children originated on the continent in the 16th century. They became particularly strong in Kent perhaps having emigrated from Holland with the weaving trade.

No more records exist for the Anabaptists. Indeed the Bishop's Visitation of 1717 reports that there are no dissenters in the parish. However the Roman Catholic element had continued. The entry in the parish register 1704 recording the death of 'Thomas Whetenhall Gentleman aged about 80 years buried in woollen' is a simple one. His family who no doubt attended St. Michael's as required by law continued in their father's faith. His son Henry refused to sign the oath of allegiance to William III and became a non juror and it was he who presided over the finale of the ancient Whetenhall inheritance. As a final blow to annihilate Roman Catholics the law of 1700 prohibited them from inheriting land. Thus Henry and his son Thomas sold the estate in 1714 to the Twysdens for £243.6s.6d – the price of allegiance to their faith.[8] Other property such as Goose Green Farm remained but this was not ancient entail and was sold off at a later date.[9] Perhaps this cleared the air for St. Michael's. The Visitation of 1717 reports one family of Roman Catholics and two women and in the later Visitation of 1759 there were two papists, a widow and her daughter who live on a farm. *'They are attended at their own house by an itinerant priest. All her sons are men of the Church of England'*. Thomas (who sold the estate) is said to have died in Brussels in 1768 and his death terminated the East Peckham branch of the Whetenhall family. His brother Henry became Friar Henry Whetenhall of the Society of Jesus, and died in London in 1745. A third brother James, a secular priest became confessor to the English Benedictine Nuns at Ghent while one sister became Dame Catherine Maura Whetenhall Order of the Society of Benedict of Brussels and another sister became Dame Mary Placida Whetenhall O.S.B. of Pontoise.[10]

References

1   PCC Admin. vol VI, 1631–1648.
2   A modern translation of the memoirs with commentary by Peter Quennell was published by Routledge in 1930. The bad reputation which Hammond gave Elizabeth Whetenhall is shown to be inaccurate. His account of the Court frivolities at Tunbridge Wells in 1666 in which he involves her does not take into consideration that she died 1664!
3   BL Add Ms 421 The Voyage of Lady Catherine Whetenhall.
4   The grave and epitaph was covered when the floor of the church was renewed in the 18c. Fortunately the inscription was recorded and preserved. It is included in Don Guido Beltmore's, The History and Art in the Church of Saint Thomas the Martyr Padua, published 1966 by Tipographical Antoniana. It is written in very flowery, poetic semi classical Latin all of which is not quoted. I am very grateful to C.D. Humphery-Smith of the Institute of Genealogical Studies, Canterbury for his co-operation in tracing this information in Padua, after my failed two year search, and for translating the epitaph.
5   J.S. Cockburn. Calendar of Assize Records Kent indictments Charles II 1676–1688.
6   LLP Compton Census 1676 VH 72/9
7   LLP Ms 1391 Correspondence between Twysden and Whetenhal.
8   CKS U55 T315 sale of Whetenhall estate.
9   CKS TR1335/2 Oxonhoathe Estate Book.
10 CRS 1909 vol 7 The Bedingfield Papers.

4. Peckham Under Four Georges

In retrospect the church can be seen to have come through a stormy passage but no one could have predicted the actual physical storm which struck the church during The Great Storm of 1703, the worst in British history. On November 26th and 27th winds estimated at more than hurricane force occurred with gusts reaching 120mph. Daniel Defoe, best known for his book Robinson Crusoe, described how 8,000 men were lost at sea, ships around the coast were smashed and almost every ship on the Thames was destroyed or damaged, thousands of trees uprooted, 17,000 in Kent alone. Streets were said to be filled with rubble from fallen masonry. Those who experienced the hurricane of 1987 may appreciate the effect on the farms and homesteads of East Peckham but in 1704, in addition to damage to property and crops, the steeple of the church was toppled. According to Daniel Defoe, in his collection of stories about the storm, an eyewitness, the Vicar of Brenchley, estimated that St. Michael's spire was as tall as that of Brenchley which had also been blown down.[1]

In May 1704 Churchwarden Thomas Long in his annual report to the Bishop says, in what might be considered an understatement, that there was nothing to report *'saving our church being out of repair which we shall repair as soon as conveniently we can'*. This is enlarged in October 1704 by Churchwarden John King, *'whereas our steeple suffered much by the Great Storm care is taken for the repair of it'*, and in May 1705 Churchwardens Jordan Gilbert and John Kipping report triumphantly that *'whereas our church suffered extremely by the great storm to a great cost and charge of the parishioners the damage is now fully repaired'*. The church shared in the national distress caused by the storm. On October 4th 1704 it was reported that the vicar *'payde Mr. Tylott by my church wardens ye brief for seaman's widows whose husbands were cast away in ye great storm – 16s.8d'*. Briefs were Royal letters patent requiring collections for special purposes and were read out in church before the sermon. Fortunately there were no local casualties as the burial register has no entries for November 1703.

How tall the original spire was will never be known with certainty but with shrewdness, to avoid the accident ever recurring, and suspiciously, to avoid the cost, only the existing spirelet was built. To mark the historic occasion a weather vane was mounted bearing the date 1704.[2]

Some indication of the height of the spire is suggested by a writer at the time who described the Brenchley spire as *'a stately steeple whose altitude exceeded almost, if not all in Kent. The height whereof according to various computations, it never in my knowledge being exactly measured, did amount at least to ten rods, some say twelve and others more, yet this strong and noble structure by the rage of the winds was leveled to the ground ... some houses and some barns with other buildings are quite demolished'*.[3 and 4]

After he was consecrated in 1758 Archbishop Secker wanted a detailed knowledge of the clergy and parishioners newly under his charge. The vicar's replies to a printed questionnaire which Secker sent to each incumbent in the Diocese of Canterbury and, fortunately, to those in the

Deanery of Shoreham, outlines the local picture and shows how church routine had developed and settled since the upheavals of the previous two centuries. There was not a single member of another sect in the parish, nor was there a dissenter or any person who absented themselves from church out of a professed disregard for religion. The only remnant from earlier times were those previously mentioned *'two Papists, a widow and her daughter, who live on a farm and are attended at their own house by an itinerant priest'.*

There were about two hundred houses and cottages. The roads were bad and about three quarters of the people lived more than two miles from the church. *'Yet there is a large congregation and all the people of substance of whom there are many attend constantly and the rest as often as they can'.* Those children being prepared for confirmation were taught the faith, the 'catechism' once a week during the six weeks of Lent.

The standard liturgy for the period was firmly adhered to. There was *'a whole service'* on Sundays, Prayers on Ash Wednesday, Good Friday, Christmas Day and St. Stephen's. The sacrament of the Lord's supper was administered at each of the great festivals, Christmas, Easter, Whitsun and the Sunday following each of those festivals and on two Sundays near Michaelmas.

The vicar Henry Hall reports that *'when I have been there at those times I have found fifty communicants'.*

His absence at other times was due to the fact that he was a pluralist. This often arose from the system whereby a vicar could hold two or more neighbouring small parishes residing in one of them and serving the other personally. But an even worse situation, which obtained at St. Michaels' occurred where the parishes were at a distance from each other and a curate was employed to do the work on a much reduced salary. The situation was further aggravated by the fact that the Archbishop of Canterbury had the patronage with the right to appoint his own nominee as vicar who had the income from the Small Tithe. Although the practice operated in the medieval period it is in the Georgian period that the evidence becomes prominent.[6] There was a list of eminent churchmen, who were already drawing a stipend from the revenue of the Cathedral as members of the controlling Chapter, known as Prebends, while receiving an income from St. Michael's and other places in the archbishop's gift.

Henry Hall, who reported the Visitation, states that he resides on his own living at Harbledown. *'The cure of East Peckham is served by Mr. Austin Gammon in Deacon's orders who resides in the vicarage house. I allow him £40 per annum'.* Henry Hall was also Librarian to the Archbishop of Canterbury, Rector of the sinecure of Orpington and the Treasurer of Wells Cathedral.

Other pluralists who were rectors of East Peckham were:

Figure 18. A drawing found in Church papers shows the now defaced sundial in a happier age.

1719 **William Bradshaw**, Prebend of Canterbury and afterwards Bishop of Bristol.

1751 **Francis Walwin**, Prebend of Canterbury. He held St.Mary Bradshaw Canturbury. He resigned that on being presented to Adisham; and following him were

1763 **John Davis**, Doctor of Divinity, Prebend of Canterbury. Rector of Hannsey, Sussex where he lived.

1766 **William Tatton**, Prebend of Canterbury, Rector of Rotherfield. He resigned this on being presented to St. Dionysis, Backchurch, London.

1775 **George Berkley**, Doctor of Law, Prebend of Canterbury, Vicar of Cookham in Berkshire where he lived. He was the son of the Bishop of Clayne.

1787 **Richard Lucas**, Doctor of Divinity, Prebend of Canterbury.

1789 **Thomas Vyner**, Doctor of Divinity, Prebend of Canterbury and Rector of Fankton, Warwickshire STP.

This culminated in 1805 with the appointment of George Moore, the son of the Archbishop of Canterbury, Prebend of Canterbury Cathedral, Rector of Wrotham and Stanstead. He was also Registrar of the Prerogative Court of Canterbury which presided over the proving of wills. Eight curates were to serve under him at St. Michael's including the Rev. Lambert Larking who became a well known antiquarian and founder of the Kent Archaeological Society in 1857.[5]

But in spite of this absenteeism there is no sign of neglect. The church was exceptionally well served by its vicars and curates. Valentine Chadwick (1689–1719) reporting to the bishop in the Visitation of 1717 says that he has known the people well for 30 years. John Hedges served as curate and vicar for 30 years and George St. John Mitchell for 21 years. It appears from the 1805 Visitation that because many of the congregation lived a considerable distance from the church it was the custom when taking communion to the sick for the old and infirm in that area to attend. Sometimes as many as ten people were present. The church bells were serviced in 1742. The church was kept in repair with the churchwardens reporting in 1763 that *'We have supplied, remedied and repaired all such defects as were marked at the side of the article of enquiry delivered to us at the Easter Vestry. Robert Biggenden and Thomas Martin'*. Perhaps it was at this time that the church stable was built.[6]

The appearance of the Georgian church can be pictured through gleanings from various sources. A bill shows that the church door was painted white while the sundial over the entrance porch was quite a handsome sight. A later Church Warden's bill of 1832 was for *'new facing the sundial, writing gold letters shading, lining and varnishing'*. Within the porch there is evidence of Georgian graffiti on the walls.

Inside the church, on the north wall, though previously hung over the south door where the shadow can still be seen, were the Royal Coat of Arms dated 1740.

The Royal Arms had first been ordered to be displayed in churches by Henry VIII as a reminder that the King was now the Head of the Church in England. They were removed during the Commonwealth but reinstated after the Restoration. They were recognised as an expression of loyalty to the Establishment. While the date of 1740 is puzzling it was after all only thirteen years after the accession and allowing for human nature, the commissioning and the painting...! In its prime it was a colourful addition to the church.[7]

There was a gallery at the west end of the church. Evidence for this structure is a Church Warden's payment to John Rhodes for:

'Wite washing done on the side walls in the gallerys and under the gallerys and on the north side and the ceiling under the gallerys'.

These galleries at the west end were a common feature of the period. They were raised about mid century to accommodate church musicians who provided the music before church organs were generally installed. It was usual for the congregation to turn to face the musicians. When Churchwardens' accounts can be referred to at a later date they surely affirm to what must previously have been practiced. There are snippets referring to the music; Psalm singers were paid £1.16s for the half year, and Thomas Burr was paid 8 times at 2s.6d for attending at East Peckham church to instruct the singers. A bassoon was purchased at £2.12s.6d. The singers were also treated to an annual dinner. There was thus considerable community involvement in the musical aspect of Sunday worship. As would be expected the standards of these instrumental and vocal offerings varied considerably but they were probably of a good standard owing to the payment for instruction. This type of West Gallery music has recently been revived from Georgian manuscripts. Tradition was strong for when the Victorians re styled the church the present choir stalls were still placed at the west end in front of the organ.

In addition there was a gallery at the west end of the church to seat the children. Many of these children are not to be found in the baptism records for they were not born in East Peckham. Most of them were given birth under difficult conditions and were baptised the Sunday following their admission to the Foundling Hospital in London which cared for the maintenance and education of deserted and exposed young children (see later, The Foundlings).[8]

A prominent figure was the church Beadle wearing *'a super blue laced coat'* and *'a gold laced beadles' hat'* and carrying his wand of Office. In Georgian times long term holders of the Office were members of the Ellis family who continued in the office until 1900. Their duties seem to have been concerned with order in the church. On the altar shone the original church silver of unknown date because it was subsequently stolen and replaced in 1794. From his stand on what was probably a three decker pulpit, given in 1637 by Judge Thomas Twisden brother of Sir Roger, the vicar could oversee the assembled congregation.

Below the children's gallery, which seemed to be of some antiquity because it became dilapidated and needed replacement,

Figure 19. Sir William Twysden, brother of the Bishop of Raphoe, enteretained a guest the night before the fatal incident. Original at Bradbourne, East Malling. (By permission of Kent Archaeological Society).

seating in the church was most likely provided by family box pews for the *'people of substance'* and by benches for the 'rest'.[9]

Seated in their aisle were the Twysden family and their domestic household. Probably missing from their number and seeking other employment was the servant who was the link in the chain which led to the death in 1752 of Philip Twysden, the Bishop of Raphoe. As a young man Philip had entered the church and was soon to have domestic tragedy in the death of his young wife

Figure 20. Little Roydon. Site of the medieval rectory. Rebuilt 1700. Referred to in later deeds of property as Parsonage farm.

in childbirth. She was buried in St. Michael's chancel with her baby boy in her arms[10] Recovering from his grief and still it seems a charming and handsome man who became very popular in Society, he attracted the attention of Lord Chesterfield who when he became Lord Lieutenant of Ireland invited Philip Twysden to accompany him as his chaplain. So impressed was Chesterfield that in 1743 he further offered Philip the Irish Bishopric of Raphoe at the early age of 33 years. It was the same year that he remarried. From this point he and his wife appear to have led an extravagant social life and when he died in 1751 he was a bankrupt. It was no doubt his desperate financial situation that led him to the alternative occupation of 'moonlighting' as a highwayman for it is clear that he had practised on more than one occasion before the fatal incident. The following story can only be recounted in the words of the family historian who in spite of social conjecture at the time, appeared to think it was the truth.

> *'Sir William* (Philip's brother) *was very hospitable in receiving strangers at Roydon Hall who were belated on the road. One night a London doctor driving from Hastings to London, found himself belated near Roydon, drove there, was hospitably received and spent a lively evening. Bishop Twysden who was then staying in the house was present.*
>
> *In the night the doctor was awakened by the sound as of a man in pain. Going out of his room into the passage he found one of the men servants ill and in great pain. The doctor had remedies with him and relieved the man. In the morning the man tried to speak to him privately but had no time to say any more than 'look to your pistols'. The doctor thought nothing of the warning at the time as he knew his pistols were loaded, but when driving in the coach it occurred to him to examine them. He found the charges had been drawn and he quietly reloaded the pistols.*
>
> *Presently the coach got upon Wrotham Heath. Two masked men rode up and stopped the coachman. One of them pointed the pistol at the doctor and said, 'I shall shoot you if you move'. The doctor pointed his pistol at the man and said 'I will shoot you if you come nearer!' The man came up quickly and fearlessly – the doctor fired – the man fell dead. The doctor got out of his coach to examine the dead man, removed the mask and found he was the Bishop, the brother of his host the previous night'.*[11]

It would appear that the family not unnaturally tried to conceal the circumstances of the Bishop's death. The St. Michael's register enters *'Buried Bishop of Raphoe'* which is the proof of his burial place. The family historian claims that he was buried in the churchyard but there is no gravestone to such an eminent person nor is there a monumental inscription in the church. His first wife had been buried in the chancel because at that time the Twysdens held the privileged lease of the Parsonage with its responsibilities towards the chancel.

Also taking their seats in the chancel were the Henham family. Their family historian claims to trace their genealogy to medieval Europe, in fact to the Emperor Charlemagne in 800. Certainly they had a long Kentish ancestry with the East Peckham branch beginning in 1670 when Richard Henham of Great Chart married at St. Michael's. His wife Mary Plane came from another Kentish family of note. Deeds of property show that they lived first at Pond Farm, Bell's Lane.[12] The historian explains their family's story in verse – that relating to East Peckham reads:

> *'He round Great Peckham grew his hops and corn,*
> *And in his yeoman state maintained his lot,*
> *And there his son, Iden, by name was born,*
> *An affix that the Henhams ne'er forgot'.*[13]

Their eldest son born 1671 was named Iden through his wife's connection with the ancient Iden family of Kent. This began a tradition continued to this day in many parts of the world – the eldest son of each generation is named Iden. The family historian also claims it was Iden who was responsible for constructing the Henham vault in the chancel where his wife was buried in 1788 aged 87 years followed by himself in 1789 aged 88 years. Their gravestone recording their details lie on the chancel floor. He was able to do this because he had secured the prestigious lease of the Parsonage.[14]

The responsibilities of the lease included *'at his own cost to repair all the Parsonage House and the chancel of the parish church of East Peckham and to provide man's meat and horse meat and lodgings twice a year, one day and one night, for the Dean Receiver, General Surveyor, Auditor, deputies, servants and horses when they survey and oversee the said Parsonage'*. He was also required to pay the vicar £40 a year. The lessee was entitled to the Great Tithe as had been established at the Dissolution of Christ Church monastery. There were once ample barns on site at the Parsonage Farm for storage. The lease remained in the Henham family for many years.

Added to the Henham memorials in the church are those in the churchyard. These are mainly those of the family members who built, a then, much larger Grove House, (Goose Green) about 1790. It was from there that the last Iden Henham emigrated at the age of 40. He arrived in Melbourne 1870 with his wife and seven children, the eldest of course named Iden. Their family crest, corresponding to that on his signet

Figure 21. The remaining part of Grove House built by the Henham family in about 1780.

ring was found inscribed on red brick, discarded in the garden, by an ancestor visiting Grove House in 1995. As prosperous hop growers they propagated the Henham hop the name of which remains in the village as applied to the residential Henham Gardens.

Also seated in the church were those who were not spiritually comfortable.

It was George St. John Mitchell who supplied the information for the Visitation report of 1786 which Dr. Lucas signed. It records the established order of church life with a regular pattern of services, two on Sundays with one sermon, and the Lord's Supper administered eight times a year with fifty people receiving it at a time. As the curate of the parish in priests' orders George St. John Mitchell said he resided in the parish and also served Nettlestead. He was paid £50 per annum. But there is a flicker of change in the pedestrian rhythm of parish life – an awakening of education. There is a voluntary charity school for 20 boys and girls and two Sunday schools attended by a hundred boys and girls. Although the curate reports that there are no Dissenters in the parish and that he did not think *'there was anything extraordinary relating to the parish whereof to give Your Grace information'* he was perhaps not diligent in observation for there were those in the parish who were later to identify themselves as dissenters.

It was almost 50 years since John and Charles Wesley, ministers in the Church of England, had experienced personal conversions later expressed thus in the words of Charles:

> *'My chains fell off, My heart was free*
> *I rose went forth, And followed thee'.*

As a result he and his brother spent their future lives in evangelistic work Although they remained members of the Church of England their followers separated and set up new independent churches on the evangelical principles which Wesley taught. As well as his widespread influence in the country John was especially well known locally, having friends in the Sevenoaks and Shoreham areas.

The Vicar George Moore reports in his 1805 Visitation that some Methodists professing the principles of Wesley had been introduced into the parish over the last 15 years They had a licensed meeting house and that although the curate Mr. Mitchell thought their number decreased the best informed farmers reported differently and added that they had extreme difficulty in keeping their labourers from attending the meeting house and that this was only accomplished by refusing them parochial relief if they did not attend the church.

Rev. Moore's reference to 15 years earlier refers back to 1790. It seems that a group of people in East Peckham were so sure of their new allegiance and were so well established by 1798 that they *'being part of a congregation of dissenters calling themselves Methodists'* applied to the magistrates as they were required by law so to do *'for the house of William Moore the Carpenter to be licensed as a place set aside for the worship of Almighty God'*.

But the labourers who were experiencing these difficulties had the support of influential people in the parish. Elizabeth Stanford, a wealthy widow, one of the signatories of the application, was of the centuries old yeoman family and Thomas Welfear was another substantial land owner. When Thomas died in 1851 he asked for his testimony to be used in his obituary notice in the Methodist Magazine. He vividly describes how *'About the year 1785 the fear of God was firmly implanted in my heart. There was an evening lecture at a little church in Nettlestead by a Minister who had been formerly of the Weslyean connection. I was led to think seriously. About this time the Methodists were*

Figure 22. Simon Doyle from Australia stands by the graves of his Henham ancestors.

Figure 23. The Henham Crest. Brick plaque found in garden during renovations in 1995. Identified by Simon Doyle's family signet ring.

invited to preach in East Peckham and I readily attended. From hearing them preach and having the opportunity to converse with them I felt these were the people I had been seeking for. In answer to prayer, as in the case of Cornelius, the Lord had sent them to give me further instruction. My father and those about me signified that there was no need to make such a do about religion and persecution arose but none of these things moved me '.

Thomas' recollection of the date is vague. Nonetheless the fact is that he was born in 1774 at Little Mill where his father was the miller. Land Tax records show that the family moved to Burrs Oak Farm, Hale Street, in 1792 when he was 18 years old. At his father's death in 1817 he inherited the estate and from that point Burrs Oak, the Welfear's home, became associated with Methodism until the last Welfear died in 1930.

Thomas, his son, who predeceased him in 1847 witnesses to the faith on his tombstone:

'In life he was a humble follower of Christ
And in death he was enabled with sweet submission to resign all he loved below
And exercised a calm reliance in the world's atonement'.

When the congregation felt the need for a chapel to be built it was Thomas Welfear who canvassed the village for the money.

In his self composed obituary he said that he had often felt cause when attending the chapel to weep for joy that he had been raised up to be as one part of the scaffolding for the erection of the Lord's house especially when many were brought to a knowledge of the faith as it is in Jesus. He had literally been a part of the 'scaffolding' for he owned the Nettlestead brick works and contributed the very bricks for the building.

The Methodist cause posed new problems. Finance for the development of education came in 1823 through the National School Society which demanded in return for their money that the children attend Divine Service at the church each Sunday. This was unacceptable to Methodists who consequently organised their own school and proudly produced their own banner which they displayed at village events such as Hospital Sunday.[15]

However, good will must have prevailed because the Methodist school children marched in the procession at the laying of the first stone of the New Church of Holy Trinity in 1840.

At the end of the eighteenth century the settlement of the parish was much the same as it had been for previous centuries. The difference was that in common with the national trend the population was increasing. In the sixty years between 1740 and 1800 there were 158 more marriages and 1004 more baptisms entered in the parish registers than in the previous sixty years and by 1801 the first census of the population gave an official population of 1,327. This number continued to rise until a further increase of nearly three hundred between 1821 and 1831 took the population to over 2,000. Although the census shows an apparent increase in housing this was mainly due to old farmhouses and agricultural buildings being converted into several dwellings. A limited amount of cheap terraced cottages were built in the valley. Two thirds of the community were engaged in agriculture while others were tradesmen or were employed at the tannery at Little Mill or on the barges with the Medway Navigation

Figure 24. Banner confirming the date of the Methodist school, established 1823. Passing through the Pound, the occasion is probably the Hospital Sunday procession. (Picture from a post card).

Company at Branbridges. Although there was scope for work the Poor Law accounts show much unemployment sometimes due to sickness or disability.

As early as 1826 the church recognised their problems in relation to the increased population. By then the enlarged congregation was *'squeezed into remote corners and inconvenient situations'*. In view of this it was planned to increase the seating accommodation in two ways, by erecting a gallery along the north wall of the church to seat 105 people and by rebuilding and enlarging the dilapidated children's gallery at the west end of the church to accommodate the extra children. But although £100 of the required cost of £160 was collected the project was abandoned because *'it could not conveniently be carried out'*.

There was also another problem concerning the increased population. The Elizabethan Poor Law Act of 1601 had placed upon the ancient office of Church Warden of the ecclesiastical parish the responsibility of caring for the poor.

The Vestry, so called because the officials originally met in the church vestry where the clergy donned their vestments, had become the village government, more meaningful to parishioners than central government in London. The officers who were unpaid, were elected annually by their fellow rate payers who were substantial householders and gentlemen of the parish.

The office of Overseer of the Poor had the responsibility for calling a Vestry meeting to raise a poor rate for the year, to collect the money from those who could afford to pay and to make a list of those who could not afford to do so, keeping the accounts of money both as received and paid out. The money was spent on caring for the poor, the unemployed, widows, paying for medical expenses for the sick, apprenticing orphaned children and burying the pauper dead. They also controlled the movement of the population by sending people back to their parish of origin if they became dependent on East Peckham parish. They had been required to provide accommodation and employment for the poor in a village workhouse, the earliest being at The Bull House, a former drinking house at Snoll Hatch, before moving to premises at the Bush.

Another Officer was the Surveyor of Highways, who was appointed to make and collect a highways rate for the maintenance of the parish roads.

The Vestry men were also responsible for maintenance of law and order in the parish and were required to appoint a parish constable, previously known as the Borsholder, an ancient office. All the business was recorded by the Vestry Clerk in the Vestry Book or in the appropriate accounts. Most regrettably the early records of East Peckham have long since been destroyed. Those which have survived are in the care of the Centre for Kentish Studies.

It seems that new arrangements were needed to cope with the escalating administration because the Churchwardens enter in 1829:

'Accounts for materials for the New Vestry Room.
2 horses and a man and a boy fetching water for mortar for the new vestry room.
John Hunt and William Coster were paid 2s a day.
Beer for the men was supplied.
John Leeds for carpenter's work at the vestry was paid £44.11s.5d
Thomas Bishop for bricklayers work £11.15s.8d'

There was also a bill for the stove, a fender, fire irons and a coal scuttle and chairs. Although much altered in recent years many features remain in the room.

It is to this room that 'the poor' went to receive their allowance after a long walk from the south or west of the parish. It was recorded by Rev. Ryley in 1921 that 'some years before Mrs. Golding died, she had told him that when poor relief was given on Sunday afternoon in the Vestry by the churchwardens the door of the Vestry leading into the churchyard was specially made so that those who entered by the other door should not know what the rest got. A man was posted outside to prevent any collusion'. This door is now bricked in.

Figure 25. Well Cottage, Snoll Hatch. Originally part of The Bull, a Tudor ale house. It was later used by the Parish as the village workhouse before it moved to the Bush to what is now the Fireplace shop and adjoining property. The well in the foreground gives the cottage it's name. (See also name of adjoining cottages, Bull Row). The notice remaining on the wall reads: Anyone committing a nuisance on these premises will be prosecuted according to the law. Photo given J. McCunnal.

The enlarged congregation continued to cause problems. The Churchwardens made another attempt to increase seating accommodation and in 1835 authorised *'the drawing of plans and making estimate of the cost for the construction of galleries'* but again they were not carried out.

It also brought parking problems and by 1835 the church stable was doubled in size.[16]

The burden of the Highways Surveyor's work continued to be considerable. Employed on the road were 17 men and 3 boys. Stone needed to be carted from the quarry and broken for repairs to the roads, earth needed to be moved, the three turnpike gates at Hale Street, (near Burrs Oak Farm) Seven Mile Lane (corner of Martins Lane) and Branbridges (near the Bell) needed to be kept in repair. The Churchwardens also had the responsibility for vermin control and they paid for the destruction of sparrows and their eggs as well as organising the Sparrow Club to encourage the work because flocks of sparrows could ruin the harvest. The necessity is highlighted in 1820 by the payment of £4.3s.6d for 305 dozen sparrow heads which is 3,660 heads and in the following year the payment between April and June was for 434 dozen or 5,208 heads. They were also responsible for controlling moles in the churchyard.

Some relief came to the Vestry with the passing of the New Poor Law in 1835 which closed the benevolent village workhouse at the Bush (now the Fireplace shop and adjoining property) in favour of the new Union Workhouse at West Malling. This relieved them of the responsibility of its administration and the care of up to 50 inmates. However they were still responsible for care of the able bodied unemployed.

But whatever the changes St. Michael's remained the focal point for spiritual life and for much social administration through the efforts of those substantial parishioners who constituted the Vestry.

The increasing problem of accommodation could not be ignored and the situation reached its climax when the Churchwardens called a meeting of the parishioners on New Year's Day 1840.

References

1 Daniel Defoe. 'The Storm. A Collection of the most remarkable casualties and disasters which happened in the late dreadful tempest both by land and sea'.
   Michael Brayne. 'The Greatest Storm'. Sutton 2002.
2 The weather vane in evidence today is the replacement of 1928. It was decided then that the new vane should retain the historic date of 1704.
3 Thomas Figg. Highways and Byeways in Kent 1908.
4 The soaring height of Barming's splendid church spire can be observed from the Maidstone–Tonbridge Road. Recently surveyed it measures 105ft. Even at the Vicar of Brenchley's most modest estimate of St. Michael's spire, 10 rods, =165 ft, this must be considered an interesting but exaggerated estimate. The help of Mr. Earl, Churchwarden of Barming is acknowledged. There is a local legend that the steeple fell into the field south east of the church because the field was called Steeple field. However Steeple field is referred to in 1638 long before the storm. See CKS U48 E7. Perhaps it is a corruption of steep hill.
5 Guide to the Bishops' Registers of England and Wales.
6 See later Church Stables.
7 See later The Royal Arms.
8 See later the Foundlings.
9 The suggestion that there were box pews which were replaced comes from the Visitation of 1864 when it was reported that by disposing of the gallery and re-seating the church they had been able to obtain upon the ground the same number of sittings.
10 CKS U1823/105 Z27 Lambert Larkin papers.
11 JR Twisden. The Family of Twysden and Twisden 1939.
12 CKS U47/17 T52 Pond Farm.
13 KAS Library. Genealogical Record of the Families of King and Henham 1899.
14 CKS 1163 T13 Lease of Parsonage to Henham.
15 Peter Morgan. East Peckham Methodist Church 1798–1998.
16 See later, Church Stables.

5. The Victorian Church

It was in the schoolroom (now the Retreat bungalow in Bullen Lane) that the churchwardens called a parish meeting on January 1st 1840 to consider the propriety of moving the church to the centre of the village. The reasons given for this were outlined by the Committee in an address. They said that East Peckham now had a population of 2,250, but only 500 of them could be seated at one time in its church. This stood on a high hill two and a quarter miles from the village. The aged and infirm who lived below the hill could not reach the church and in bad weather only a very few people who had a conveyance could conveniently attend it but in fine weather the congregation was numerous. The parish, they continued, was on the Medway and many of the men were employed on the river and when they came from their work on Sunday morning they lived at too great a distance from the church to be able to attend. The mothers of young children could not leave them long enough to be able to walk to church so that as long as they had the care of a family they were prevented from joining in divine worship as were domestic servants who could not without difficulty be spared the time necessary to attend church if their masters also wished to go. The parishioners universally desired to remove the evils arising from these various causes; they regret that the attendance at church is disproportionate to the population; that the aged and infirm were entirely

Figure 26. The isolated position of the Church.

deprived of the comforts of public worship and that others passed the best years of their lives without the comforts and advantages of the means of grace. For these reasons a subscription had already been opened and already half the money required had been collected. However it was decided that *'it was not proper to remove the church but that it was expedient to build a chapel of ease nearer the bulk of the population'*.

What followed this decision has been recounted in detail in an earlier publication (see Margaret Lawrence, 'The New Church'). Although at first only the daring chapel of ease was envisaged, with alternate Sundays at the two churches, suddenly the whole vision was changed when Mr. Thomas Hugh Boorman of Brixton, late of East Peckham and of the Medway Navigation Company, offered financial support for a minister for the new church provided that two full services were performed there on each Sunday throughout the year. This offer meant that the New Church of Holy Trinity was to be the parish church of a new district formed out of the ancient St. Michael's parish. It was a decision that was to alter the history of East Peckham, culminating in 1973 with the redundancy of St. Michael's church.

The success of the venture can be demonstrated by the figures taken for the 1851 Religious Census. The attendance at St. Michael's on Sunday March 30 1851 was 70 plus 52 children in the morning and 85 plus 47 children in the afternoon. That at Holy Trinity was far greater, 213 plus 126 children in the morning and 200 plus 100 children in the afternoon.[1]

But although it has been suggested that after the new church was built St. Michael's became neglected, nothing could be further from the truth. On February 2nd 1864 The Maidstone Journal reports the opening of the parish church for divine worship after careful restoration carried out by loving reverent hands.

It recalls that *'in 1857 the owners of the chancel and adjoining mortuary chapel set the example. Those portions of the building were restored. Each of the four arches were entirely rebuilt and the floors paved with Minton tiles. Two valuable painted windows were inserted, one by O'Connor to the memory of the late William Cook (Jun.) Esq and one by Warrington to the memory of the late Thomas Hugh Boorman Esq.*[2] *Since then nine of the most decayed of the old windows have been reinstated. But in the early part of last year (1863) the present larger work had been taken in hand, and after many hindrances in the course of the work they had been at length completed'*.

The writer goes on to record the restoration, a valuable record for future historians. The floor was raised by one step and the surface was concreted. Parts of the walls were underpinned and all the walls were re-plastered. Woodwork was given special attention with the whole of the nave and the south aisle being entirely re-seated in best oak and a new pulpit and prayer desk were provided. The oak screen in the tower arch was inserted at this time no doubt to conserve the warmth from the new apparatus for warming by a hot water system and to screen the bell ringers who rang from the floor of the tower. The aisle, porch and tower were re-paved and the roof repaired where needed. More much needed light was gained by rebuilding the large west window. The previous window had been removed after it had fallen into decay and the space had been in-filled with brick. This window was principally the gift of a few friends.

At this time also the church was greatly improved by the entire renewal of the stonework and glass of the east window, the gift of the archdeacon of Maidstone. The chapel too was beautified by Mr. Cook of Roydon Hall, who inserted a painted window of much merit by Messrs Hardman, in memory of his wife who died in 1862.[2] He also removed a large unsightly pew and replaced it with two very handsome stall seats.

The report continues 'It is worthy of observation that in this church every restoration of stonework has been an exact reproduction of original work, not the attempt of an improvement of it. The cost of the repairs and new apparatus for warming by hot water was met by a subscription from some of the land owners and a few others largely assisted by a liberal contribution from T. M. Wilde and Lord Falmouth. The much heavier expenditure for the above named restorations was undertaken by two families intimately connected with the parish. The work was done under the able direction of J. Clarke Diocesan architect, the builders were Messrs. Bowley of Westminster and for the stonework Messrs Sutton and Vaughan of Maidstone'.

The strains caused by the lengthy upheaval in the church were forgotten on that day of rejoicing.

'The early morning of Wednesday gave no promise of a fine day but as the bells peeled out merrily at eight o'clock, the weather improved and the threatening clouds began to roll away as if ashamed to spoil the rejoicing of the day. Half past eleven was the time appointed for morning prayer and shortly before that time a numerous congregation assembled in the now decorously fitted building'. Those present included a band of eighteen clergy from neighbouring parishes wearing their surplices, who processed to their seats in the chancel, many county gentlemen and parish gentlemen and their wives. The singing was lead only by the village choir principally composed of young people who had been trained to their state of efficiency by the organist Mr. Jones. The congregation joined most heartily in the singing the tunes which were selected from Hymns Ancient and Modern, newly published in 1861.

'After the morning service a large party of friends partook of luncheon at Roydon Hall and the vicarage.

At six o'clock the church fully lighted for the occasion was again quite filled, this time for the most part by the poorer parishioners and their friends. The sermon was preached by the curate of Larkfield chapel who earnestly appealed to the congregation to make the restoration of their church the occasion of their own renewed earnestness in seeking those things which belonged to their peace. The collections taken at the two services amounted to £54.11s.7d. The money was given to other works not originally undertaken and especially to the urgently needed repairs to the church porch'.

This full description does not however record the significance of the 'apparatus for warming with hot water'. For the first time the congregation sat in a warm centrally heated church. This had involved a truly massive engineering work below the vestry floor in order to construct a boiler room. A depth of twelve feet of solid rock was hacked out in order to form a boiler room some twelve feet by seven in which a six foot wide brick boiler was installed with massive pipes to carry the water. The room was reached externally by steps leading down to the door. (as on plan).

Equally remarkable was the water supply needed for the system. This explains the mystery of the churchyard well outside the west door of which there is no mention in the Churchwarden's accounts until 1863 when they paid to have it cleaned out. The construction of a well through the rock was a formidable task. Both the room and the well are now sealed.

The Maidstone Journal report further reports:

'On this occasion the poor were not forgotten. In the interval between the church services a substantial dinner was provided in an oast kindly lent by Mr. Wilde at Little Roydon. It was tastefully decorated with evergreens, the work of Mrs. Tarlton, Miss L. Onslow and Miss Edith Cook.

About two hundred and thirty of the labouring men and their wives and older children were entertained. The dinner, having regard to the time of the year and the number to be provided for, was no small achievement. It consisted *of a plentiful supply of hot joints of roast and boiled beef and pork with vegetables of several sorts, followed by hot plum puddings. The whole was cooked to perfection and served to the minute.*

For this result great thanks and praise are due to the ladies of the dinner committee, especially to one by whose persevering efforts the apparent impossibility of dishing up a hot dinner were overcome and in no less a degree to the gentlemen who kindly presided at the respective tables'.

Here followed the names of parish gentlemen.

'After the feast three hearty cheers were given for the Vicar, Mr. Cook, the Founder of the Feast and the Churchwardens'.

The reporter concludes that,

'It was a pleasant sight to see so many of the sons of toil most thoroughly enjoying themselves and the day will long be remembered in the parish'.

The cheers were well deserved especially for the vicar the Rev Middleton Onslow, who had arrived in 1853 and endured eleven years of upheaval in the church building. Also there had been domestic problems at the time of his arrival because the old vicarage had been destroyed by fire after which the handsome new vicarage was built north of the old site.[3]

However the Diocesan returns for the same year 1864 fills in another side of the picture. In reply to a printed question; *'Are there any special circumstances which impede the progress of religion?'*, the vicar states that *'the great demand for female labour in the cultivation of the hops during the year … is very prejudicial'*.

The increasingly lucrative trade in the brewing industry occasioned by the increased population and the growth of the new industrial towns led to the brewers' demand for increased hop acreage from the Kentish farmers. As a result the English hop acreage doubled between 1800 and 1870. In East Peckham the Hop Tithe records show that 53 people were growing hops, the amounts varying from half an acre by the small holder to 49 acres by the largest farmer. Moreover at this point, 1862, the affluence of brewers and growers grew when profits increased through the removal of the Hop Excise duty. Clearly the vicar thought that this affluence leading to the demand for female labour was not helpful. The situation developed and by 1872 he is complaining of an evil necessarily connected with the cultivation of hops and fruit. The large demand for labour in the hop and fruit gardens was a great hindrance and took women away from their household duties and the elder boys and girls from school. Thus the women had *'much homework on Sundays and the Lord's Day was not observed as it ought to be'*. He also considered that the introduction of a large number of 'strangers' for the hop picking was not helpful.

Figure 27. The demand for labour took women away from their household duties.

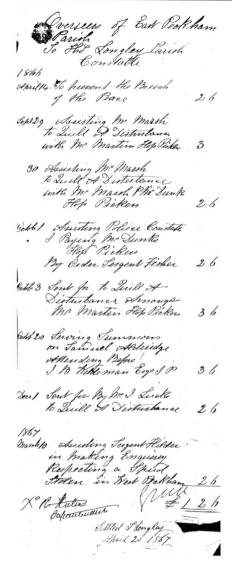

Figure 28. Overseers payment to Parish Constable 1866 'for quelling disturbance among the hop pickers'.

The 'strangers' were mainly the poor and unemployed from London who flocked to Kent in September seeking employment in this expanding industry. But the hop gardens were regarded as 'hell'. Indeed the vicar had cause for complaint for already the Constables were having to patrol the village during hopping. There are numerous Overseers' payments to the Constable *'to Quell a Disturbance'* among the hoppers at various farms.

At that time the farmers were not required to provide accommodation, sanitation, water or cooking facilities. The social problem of thousands of homeless people was ignored until Christian philanthropists campaigned for humane conditions and succeeded in obtaining local Bye Laws, dating from about 1879 according to district, which required farmers to provide basic accommodation and facilities. This brought order and comparative sobriety to the villages. In the meantime the parishes carried the burden. As the season became known as 'The Festival' it became generally accepted that not many people went to church during hopping![4]

Problems arose concerning the two new chancel roofs in spite of the recent restorations. At that time they had been redesigned and rebuilt with a new pitch. It was pointed out that they were in a bad state of repair. The new appearance was not pleasing and because of the necessary repairs it was decided to rebuild and return to the former pitch still in evidence today. (See Howard Jones, Architectural and Archaeological Appraisal).

The correspondence concerning the matter in The Church Commissioners' papers questions the financial responsibility for the repairs. By this date the Rectorial property, the Parsonage estate, had been assigned to the Dean and Chapter of Canterbury who were now responsible for the chancel and agreed to pay. It was Lady George Gordon Lennox, sister of the late William Cook, who in correspondence feared and questioned whether she was financially responsible for the repair of the south chancel (or Twysden Chapel) but she did generously pay the substantial sum. Her monument with others of the Cook family are in that chancel. She was a remarkable lady described by the vicar as a Lady Bountiful who so visited the sick and needy and supplied their needs that no alms were required from the church.

Since the Reformation the smaller chancel had been by tradition associated with Roydon Hall and is often referred to as the Twysden chapel, but there is no evidence that the Twysdens 'owned' it or paid anything for its upkeep apart from the normal church rates, or bequeathed money for its upkeep. When the Cook family bought Roydon Hall in 1835 they continued its association with the chancel providing most generously for its restoration 1857 but the question of who, or why, or how anyone actually 'owned' it remains a mystery probably lost in the medieval past! The only hatchment of the Twysden family remains on the west wall. These hatchments were displayed outside the deceased's house at the time of death and later were displayed in the church. This particular example portraying a skull indicates that this belongs to the last member of the family.

At the close of a long incumbency, the Rev Middleton Onlsow suffered the deterioration of his eyesight so that he needed the assistance of a curate to perform his church duties. Another problem was the fact that *'an increased effort had been made to induce persons to forsake their church especially by the building of a new meeting house just beyond the border of the parish to the school of which the children are enticed on Sundays'*. Unfortunately he does not state in which direction the school lay!

In spite of problems he could report in 1880 an average attendance of 120.

It was the new incumbent, the Rev. Merryweather 1883–1900, who witnessed the closing years of the century. He was an elderly man and his many references to the steep hill seems to symbolizes his attitude; *'the very steep hill prevents old people from attending'*, *'most people live nearer another church with good level roads'*. He later reports (1898) that his predecessor's sister had been found

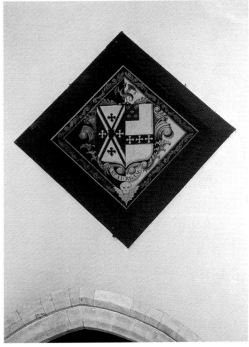

Figure 29. The Twysden Hatchment. The hatchment displaying the gentleman's heraldic arms hung outside the deceased's home for a year and was then hung in the church. The skull illustrated here is said to indicate the last of the family. © Colin Rainer.

dead on the steep hill between the vicarage and the church and his doctor had ordered that on no account was he to walk up to the church. For this reason he had asked to be able to hold his afternoon service among the people but the Bishop had required this to be held in the church yet gave permission for him to hold a third service. However he explained that as he was aged between 80 and 90 years he could not cope with a two mile walk beside (Actually he had been 66 years old when appointed to the parish and at that moment he was 81 years old and 83 when he left). Again, he does not enlarge his statement – where would he have held his afternoon service? He despairs again when reporting an average attendance of 80–100, that in a church which seated 400 it could not be filled even if every baby attended! At an advanced age he had to cope with the new administration of the Parish Council Act of 1894.[5] How the church dealt with the changed aspects in a new century best unfolds with the arrival of the Rev Ryley in 1911.

References

1   Margaret Roake. Religious Worship in Kent. The census of 1851. Kent Archaeological Society. 1999.
2   See later Victorian Stained Glass.
3   CKS CCRc E24 1853.
4   See Margaret Lawrence. The Encircling Hop. The History of the Hop and Brewing Industry.
5   See Margaret Lawrence. A Bridge Over the Stream. The History of the Parish Council 1894–1984.

6. The Twentieth Century Dawns

Geoffrey Ryley spent 18 years at St. Michael's ministering to the 349 souls recorded on the 1911 census and increasing by 25 on the 1921 census. His predecessor the Rev. Wood Loosemore had been one who had done much strenuous and valuable work in Canada between 1855–70 before returning home but when he came to East Peckham in 1900 his bodily powers shewed signs of decline and his last years were full of suffering. He was aged 79 when he was buried at St. Michael's in January 1911. He had not been able to be regularly among his parishioners. The Rev. Ryley paying tribute to him said that he was a courteous, kindly and sympathetic man. With these words, given the most charitable interpretation, it meant that the new vicar needed to give strong leadership. He found that the number of communicants was lamentably small and a blot on the spiritual life of the parish. He urged those who had lapsed in that respect to return to their parish altar. He was first and foremost aware of his vocation as a parish priest with its weighty responsibilities and asked for prayer and sympathetic help in his endeavours to live and act upon them.

Like so many of his predecessors over the centuries he was first faced with repairs to the church building. It was at this point that the tower and north wall of the nave were encased in the much regretted roman cement which hides historical detail.

One of the new vicar's assets was his musical ability. He was a Bachelor of Music, having moved in a musical atmosphere since the age of ten when he first began to play the organ. He was a close friend of the famous composer Elgar who attended choir practices when he stayed at the vicarage. Unfortunately, arrangements had already been made by 1911 for a new (the present) organ for the church and the harmonium (American organ) was put up for sale. Had the vicar been in time for the choice a more splendid instrument might have been chosen. He did however save the American organ from sale saying he 'could use it.' It remains in the church.

A new organist took up his post in 1913, one Mr. C.H. Warren of Mereworth, and it is from his pen that there exists a unique appreciation of the vicar's music. In his book, A Boy in Kent, he tells of his boyhood in the village of 'Fladmere' (Mereworth). He describes 'Mr. Stenning *'who was vicar of the neighbouring church which was perched on top of a wooded hill remote even from the cottages of its own village'.* 'Mr. Stenning' was in fact the Rev. Ryley. He had magnetic attraction but what really drew people to his church on the hill was his luscious voice. *'To hear him speak was to lose the sense of what he was saying in the music of the way he was saying it but to hear him sing was heaven itself'.* Rich and vibrant it rang through the little church sending a very pleasant tingle down the little boy's spine filling him with a kind of exultation. Geoffrey Ryley could also compose music and play the organ drawing from it the most surprising sounds even though it was a small and feeble instrument. Sometimes after Evensong he would improvise and they would stay on to hear the melting music wishing it would never cease.

Another description of the music comes from Beatrice Jeffery (nee Lewry) born 1912 who joined the choir in 1923. It was composed of 20 men, ladies and children over 11 years. They sat in the choir stalls near the organ at the west end of the church. Choir practices were occasionally enlivened by the presence of Edward Elgar who is remembered as being a rather stern old man and was well known for pulling the choir up sharply! Being a close friend of the vicar he often stayed at the vicarage but in order to preserve his privacy he was always referred to as 'my friend'.

Communication in that small rural area, made more difficult by the challenging steep hill with its crippling remoteness, had always been a problem as so eloquently described by his predecessors, but within a few months of arrival he mentally surmounted it with a few words:

'I believe it is a fact that this parish has never had a monthly magazine of its own. I think we ought to have one. I send this out in the hope and belief that it will be warmly welcomed'. The Parish Magazine was born![1] He then makes a classic understatement, *'In such a small parish as ours it is obvious that there will not be much to chronicle'.* He did not know that he would be chronicling the effect of a world war on his 'small parish'.

The First World War

The magazines for the summer days of July and August 1914 read with the usual happy atmosphere of English parish affairs; the sun shone, the new churchyard was due to be opened, Bertha Simmons had been presented with a silver watch to mark seven years unbroken school attendance marking seven years of good conduct, perseverance and determination, and there was mention of workers in the fields and hop gardens. The school children were the guests of Colonel and Lady Villiers at Roydon Hall. The approach of the procession from the school was heralded by the strains of music delivered by East Peckham brass band. There were games for the girls, a cricket match for the boys, a dolls house and other entertainment for the infants. There were more games, balloons and a football match, tug o' war, sack racing, donkey rides and of course tea and before going home they enjoyed a singsong. *'A thoroughly enjoyable afternoon was spent'.*

The choir's annual outing to the seaside took place. Belatedly because the driver had searched Hadlow in vain for St Michael's school! After the lovely two hour drive to Eastbourne the day was spent paddling, motor boat riding, shopping, eating and finally enjoying a liberal tea. On return the National Anthem was struck up as they approached the school where amid much cheering the party broke up. There was even more. The Sunday school had its annual treat. Fifty children were invited to Grove House by Mr. and Mrs. Elvin. A cricket match, games and races preceded tea which was served on the lawn. A *'profusion of comestibles kept every mouth busy for an hour'.* There were ices and prizes and each child had a bag of lollipops to take home.

Dated August 17th and printed in the September issue are the words which spoke the change to this happy world. They came as a shock to a parochial community, mostly unaffected by the outside world and without the media of our present day. Very few were as yet even affected by owning a wireless.

'There is no need for me to dilate on the awful thing which has happened since I last wrote. We have all of us, I trust made up our minds to face the terrible situation into which we have been forced in true English spirit. This war is going to be a supreme test of our endurance as a nation and as individuals. There is not one of us who is not going to feel the effects of it, but if we are true

sons and daughters of Britain we shall calmly, bravely, resolutely and cheerfully bear our burden and put ourselves out to bear another's burden'.

Almost immediately the effect of the war was felt in this small community. In the following issue three men, Privates Butchers, Payne and Sharman had joined Lord Kitchener's army and ten other men were serving as regular members of the army and navy. Petty Officer Frank Pay serving on Submarine E9 took part in and survived two early successful encounters with the German navy.

Then came the shattering news that brought home that they were indeed going to be affected by the war. Colonel Edwin Berkely Cook son of Ralph Cook of Roydon Hall passed away on November 4th from wounds received in the battle near Messines. *'No parish ever had a better friend. How greatly he was loved was abundantly shown on the day of his funeral; the crowd in the church which included officers and men of the first Life Guards in uniform, the solemnity of the internment in the churchyard and the half muffled peal of bells. He took an intense practical interest in the various branches of parochial life'.* Great sympathy was expressed to the Cook family who planned a memorial to their son which was dedicated at a very impressive and emotional service described in the later magazine of August 1917 together with a description of the memorial. It consisted of the altar and reredos which remains in the church.

> *'The altar and reredos each of oak are beautiful specimens of wood carving. At the foot of the altar the following Latin inscription is carved – AD MAJOREM DEI GLORIAM (to the greater glory of God). The top is covered by a lovely deep crimson velvet, edged with gold fringe which falls over the front and sides, two fair linen cloths have also been provided. The reredos stretches the length of the east wall and consists of a pinnacled centre piece and wings. The super altar is fixed to the centre piece. The ornaments, a brass cross for which an alcove surmounted by a canopy has been provided, brass candlesticks and flower vases are massive and of exquisite design and are with the velvet and linens the gift of Mr. Ralph Cook.*
>
> *At the foot of the wings has been carved the following inscription:*
> *"In memory of Edwin Berkely Cook of Roydon Hall Lt.Colonel 1st Life Guards commanding in the original Expeditionary Force the composite Regiment of (on the south wing) Household Cavalry. Died Nov 4 th 1914 of wounds received in action near Messines Oct 21st. Erected by members of his family. Mr. and Mrs. Ralph Cook, Mrs. Possomby, Mrs. Stapleton, Sir Frederick Cook and Mr. Herbert Cook"'.*

Throughout the war the Rev. Ryley writes in detail of those who are serving with the intent that they should be remembered individually in prayer. By August 1916 the list of those serving had grown to 35 men. Privates Basset, Carter, Sharman, Frank Skinner and H. Skinner had been wounded. By October H. Bell of Court Lodge had been wounded and by December Ted Payne, one of the first to respond to the call of King and Country had died of wounds received in October. He had been a communicant and member of the choir and had a natural buoyancy of spirit. In writing to his mother his Commanding Officer paid a beautiful tribute to his memory. By October 1917 the list of those serving had grown to 43 men and in November it was reduced by one at the death of Second Lieutenant Francis Hart Dyke of Leavers.

'In front of me as I write there is a photograph of a pure high-souled English lad in khaki. I last saw him when he was home on leave not much more than two months ago. I shall not see him again in this world because he has passed through the gates of

Paradise.' He had been killed instantly by a shell in his dug-out on September 27th.

His death was a blow to Colonel and Mrs. Hart Dyke. They had enjoyed a tranquil domestic home life. Mrs. Emma Samson, aged 94, recalls the family procession, walking to church along the lanes from Leavers. The parents were followed by their two sons and daughter with the large domestic staff and coachman walking behind. Their son had not intended to take up the army as a profession but could not resist the call of patriotism when the war broke out. Letters were received from the front testifying that he was held in affectionate esteem by his brother officers and men. There was a tribute from the adjutant of the regiment as to his military abilities, and a letter from the Captain of his Company saying that professionally he was never anything but good *'but it is off parade that he will be most missed. He was so modest and friendly and would go anywhere and do anything. He was truly a perfect English gentleman.'* But nowhere was his death more keenly felt than in his home village and at his memorial service in St.Michael's church. Later a memorial in veined alabaster was placed on the south wall bearing simple but stark words:

'In thankful memory of Francs Hart Dyke 2nd Lieut. Royal West Kent Regiment who laid down his life for his country near Ypres in Flanders 27th September 1917 in the twentieth year of his age. Eldest son of Col. E. Hart Dyke of Leavers in this parish'.

The following month the death of Charles William Parks, one of the sailor sons of Mr. and Mrs. Parks of Bells Farm, was recorded. He was not known to many people because his parents had only recently come to live in the parish.

Sadly more deaths were to come. Most pathetically and shortly before hostilities ceased was the death of Private Jack Moon, only son of Mr. and Mrs. Moon of Goose Green who died in France in September. He had joined the army before the war broke out and served throughout being awarded the Military Medal for his *'gallantry and devotion to duty'* at the battle of Messines – only later to die in hospital from the effects of a gas shell wound. His young wife was sent for but arrived too late to see him alive. His service record shows him to be buried in the Mont Huon Military Cemetery in France. Sharing the same grief was a Mrs. Hobbs who had become a widow after her husband had been killed in France. Their last Sunday in England had seen the Hobbs together at the communion table.

He also records a sad encounter:

'On New Years Eve 1916 an officer who was on leave and staying in the neighbourhood walked up our way and found himself in the churchyard. He was a poet and his poetic soul was stirred by what he saw and heard. Although literary critics are not appreciative

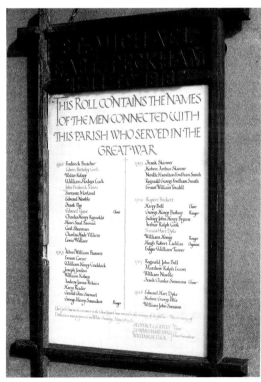

Figure 30. Roll of Honour. 'A beautiful carved oak frame'. The names of all those from St. Michael's parish who had served their country.

of his style he described in verse how he saw the lamp of day blaze out in fire leaving behind his image of the "virgin moon", who "rode bejewelled in her stately grace and flashed her message to the dying year"'.

The concluding verse was;

'I heard soft English voices rise in Psalm
Praising their maker in that village church
Then 'tween the graveyard's yew and the birch
I wondered forth; the moon had wrought her calm.'

'Some four months later this officer gallantly leading his company made the supreme sacrifice and entered the calm haven of rest.' Sadly his name was not recorded.

Like many before and since this soldier found calm here. Did he continue to hear those soft voices through the barrage of the guns?

Many names mentioned by the Rev. Ryley do not appear on the war memorial. This is because many men had association with St. Michael's in the past, were known locally but had moved. Private Hammond was born at St. Michael's and was buried in the churchyard although his parents had moved to West Malling.

One name which does appear, that of Rupert Becket, records that he was of the Hants Cyclists when he was in fact of the Huntingdon Cyclists. It is questionable if his name should appear at all. He died at the Malling Union Infirmary at West Malling in June 1918 having been discharged in 1917 as permanently unfit for military service. His service record states that he was of very poor physique, a very sick man in a very feeble condition. It is possible that he was already a sick boy when enlisted and his medical report suggests that he had been exposed to the elements during his early army life and probably was not strong enough for those rigours. The vicar writes that after he joined up he spent most of his time in hospital. *'He was a good lad, most patient in his sufferings and very appreciative of the care bestowed on him by his foster mother Mrs.Constant of Bells Farm.'*

The people turned out for an emotional service of thanksgiving at 7pm on November 12th 1918, a service called at short notice but one which drew people from their homes in gratitude for the end of the war.

It was the following July that the nation celebrated the signing of the Peace Treaty. In East Peckham the bells of St Michael's rang out during the morning and on Mill Field in the afternoon the two parishes joined together for an afternoon of sports for children and adults when there were a hundred prizes to be competed for. All was accompanied by music from the Invicta Band. There was tea for the children at Branbridge Hall which was gaily adorned with bunting, flags and flowers. Late in the evening Sir William's Hill was scaled by a large crowd in order to witness the lighting of a mighty bonfire and admiralty flares. It was a brilliant scene and a fitting termination to a day long to be remembered. The celebrations were continued the following year when an entertainment was held for the men who had returned from the war (see Margaret Lawrence, 'A Bridge Over the Stream', 1994).

Such a traumatic period could not easily be forgotten. A beautiful carved oak frame had been worked by Mr. Middleton of Peckham Bush containing a Roll of Honour – the names of all those who had served their country – which remains in the church to this day. But there was a desire for a Parish war memorial, an expression on the part of the inhabitants of the parish of their gratitude to Almighty God for the Great Deliverance and a tribute to the Glorious Dead. It was an opportunity for individuals to make a thank offering for the safe return of one whom they especially loved and also a means of commemorating a dear one whom they may have lost. As a result of several discussion meetings it was agreed by a committee that a lych gate and a plaque should be erected and ninety eight families acknowledged agreement by contributing to the cost.

'What a scene there was at old Peckham church on the afternoon of Whit Sunday 15th May 1921. The whole parish appeared to be present with the addition of large numbers from surrounding villages for the dedication of our war memorial. After a beautiful service in the church the congregation such as had been able to find accommodation within the church filed out and a procession was formed which wended its way through the north east gate and round the road at the back of the church to the space in front of the memorial. The St.Michael's group of Scouts with their drummers under the direction of their scoutmaster Miss Cook, lead the procession and eventually lined up on each side of the footway leading to the lych gate. The choir, beadle, sidesmen, churchwardens, Colonel Cornwallis, Mr. Cook, and clergy passed through the lines up to the lych gate and the ex service officers and men lined up behind the scouts. When the rest of the congregation had come to a halt the churchwardens formally opened the gates and the choir passed through and took up their positions by the harmonium. Then Colonel Cornwallis took up his stand under the lych gate and after a most inspiring address unveiled the tablet by removing the Union Jack'.*

The inspiring address was printed in the Kent Messenger. The Colonel reminded the congregation of the cost that had been paid – every hamlet and every village thrown into mourning. Just as a Boy Scout was under obligation to perform at least one kindly act a day so they were under an hourly and daily obligation to those who fought for them, and as they passed week by week under that sacred lych gate they could not fail to be reminded of it. As they gazed from that beautiful churchyard they would remember those well tended cemeteries in France where the flower of English manhood lay and would remember that they died that England might live.

Figure 31. Memorial to John Norwood VC and his kinsman John Norton Norwood. Neither men were born or lived in East Peckham. © D. Sampson.

It was a cruel day. The war was not over for Colonel Cornwallis. On the afternoon of that same day his son and heir to the Linton estate, aged 30 years, was murdered in Ireland. The Kent Messenger reported that he was killed for the simple reason that he was English. Having served through the war with courage winning the Military Cross and the Croix de Guerre he was on active service in Ireland.

Off duty, he was leaving a tennis party when the gate to the house avenue was found to be shut. On leaving the car to open it a shot rang out from the shrubbery and he fell dead. Further masked and armed men appeared and only one of the party of five men and women survived the attack.

The Rev. Ryley records a previous dedication in February 1919 to the memory of two gallant soldiers. It was erected by Mr. J.C. Norwood of Glasgow:[2]

No. 211 JULY. 1929

EAST PECKHAM.

St. Michael's Monthly Magazine

Vicar—The Rev. Geoffrey C. E. Ryley, M.A., Mus. Bac.

Wardens—Mr. R. M. Cook, Mr. W. H. Luck.

Sidesmen—Messrs. J. Allen, H. Bell, A. R. Cook, A. Sears, C. Simmons, G. Welfear.

Clerk and Beadle—Mr. W. Waghorn. **Sexton**—Mr. H. Bishop.

Organist—Mr. F. C. Simmons.

Bellringers—Messrs. W. J. Pope, J. Saunders, T. Saunders, H. Bishop, G. H. Bishop, C. Saunders, A. Sears, E. J. Butcher.

Stedman & Co. Ltd., The Abbey Press, West Malling

Figure 32. The war memorial lych gate. The new photograph which first appeared on the parish magazine, 1922.

'In memory of John Norwood, captain 5th Dragoon of Guards, V.C who fell at the battle of the Marne 8th September 1914 age 38 years. And John Norton Norwood, Second Lieutenant 4th Royal Inniskilling Fusiliers (attached 2nd) who died of wounds received in the battle of the Somme 22nd July 1916 aged 24 years. Kinsmen who constituted the sixth generation male of the yeoman family of Norwood, sometime of Stilstead in this parish.
"Nothing is here for tears, nothing to wail".'

The family were from Stilstead and had worshipped in a pew near the lectern, behind which the tablet had been placed.

John Norton Norwood was born in Partick, a town in the Glasgow area which had extensive ship building yards and engineering works. At the time of volunteering for service he was living nearby in Pollockshield which almost entirely consisted of villa residences. His service record states that he was a mechanical engineer with a good knowledge of the combustion engine. He was not able to ride a horse. In fact he was very remote from his family's yeoman roots at Stilstead.

His father was John Cheesman Norwood (a combination of two Peckham yeoman names) whose family gravestones line the path to St.Michael's door. The earliest refers to 1763. In their grief at the loss of their only son his parents wished to reunite him with a place so dear to the family. Being informed that 'their boy' had been wounded on 14th July they wrote to ask if he was slightly or seriously wounded, where was he, could they visit him? The details of his death on 22nd July from wounds received were sent in a letter from the Chaplain.

'Their boy' fell to a bomb while leading a party, maybe a platoon, of Highland Light Infantry who were in support of the Inniskillings who had lost all their own officers. He was buried in the cemetery near the 49th Casualty Clearing Station.[1]

Likewise the older John Norwood's career had been remote from his yeoman's roots although both were descended from Richard Norwood (1697–1773) who had leased Stilstead before buying it from the Twysdens of Roydon Hall. John Norwood was born at Beckenham in 1876 and after a public school and university education was commissioned into the 5th Dragoon of Guards in 1899 and was sent to South Africa. He was engaged in many well recorded operations and it was his gallantry on one such occasion that he was awarded the Victoria Cross. The action took place at Bell Spruit on October 30th 1899 in the defence of Ladysmith. John, then aged 23 years, set out with a party of NCOs and men from his regiment in an attempt to meet up with a force which had been sent out from the town the previous

night, but approaching a ridge they came under heavy fire. When 600 yards from the ridge Norwood turned back his patrol and galloped off at speed. As they did so one man, Private Monnier, was hit and dropped. Norwood rode back 300 yards to where the man lay, dismounted, picked him up, put him over his shoulder and carried him back leading his horse with the other hand. All this was under incessant fire from the Boers.

Figure 33. Domestic Service at the Vicarage. Rev. Ryley with 'Julia' in the middle, Ivy Sampson, the Between Maid, left and Edith Gibbs, the Parlour Maid. Loaned by Emma Sampson

At the end of the South African War he received other awards for outstanding service and continued his military career until he resigned his commission in 1909. Even then he joined the Reserve of Officers and rejoined the 5th Dragoon Guards in August 1914 and was immediately in action in France. It was on his birthday 8th September that he and his men came under heavy fire during the Battle of the Marne at Sablonnieres. Thirteen men were wounded, two privates were killed as were the Senior Officer, Captain Partridge and John Norwood. His body was buried at Sablonnieres Communal Cemetery and his name appears on his home war memorial at Haywards Heath, Sussex. A connection has been kept by the Norwood family. The Churches Conservation Trust acknowledges in their Annual Report 1999–2000 a bequest to St. Michael's Church from Charles C. Norwood of Glasgow.

It is most unlikely that either of these men ever set foot in St. Michael's church.

After the opening of the war memorial the remaining eight years of the vicar's life at St Michael's saw the revival of parish life all of which he

Figure 34. Domestic service at Roydon Hall. The Cook family livery. Loaned by Emma Sampson.

Figure 35. Interior of church before the First World War. The Cook memorial altar and reredos and the Norwood memorial on pillar are not in place. Note oil lamps.

reported in the magazine. For him there was no partition between secular and spiritual. The Women's Institute, the Scouts, the Wolf Cubs, the Roydon Cricket Club, the football team, the Killingrove Rangers, the Invicta band, the Crowhurst Hop Mission, the East Peckham Gardeners Society, the County Library, the Girl Guides, were all mentioned in his monthly letter.

He explained later in the magazine of February 1929 how deep his roots were in 'this dear parish' and how hard it would be to go when the time came. Yet there was a point when it might be in the best interest of a parish if the vicar was to leave. The solution to his heart searching problem was suddenly solved. The Bishop of Rochester asked him to go to Rochester to act as his domestic chaplain and he accepted. After his induction in July he was known as Canon Ryley. In his farewell letter to his 'Dear Friends' he refers to their most intimate relationship. He had shared in their joys and sorrows and they had shared in his. He was no doubt referring to the joy of his marriage in 1915 and the death of his young wife in 1921, aged 31, after much suffering. He later returned in 1947 to be buried with her in the churchyard.

Reference
1 Parish Magazines 1911–1939.
2 It was indeed erected by the Glasgow family. The descendants of John Norwood have correspondence from Glasgow concerning the proposed memorial to which John's distressed wife did not reply. The name was added without her consent.

7. Between the Wars

Writing in the parish magazine for January 1932 the Rev. Partridge foretells:

'The new year is bound to bring new conditions of living and fresh changes in our social life and what we have to do is first to understand them and then to face them, adapting ourselves to them with all the courage and wisdom that lie within our power'.

His prediction was for that year but with hind sight it could be seen to cover the events of the next seven years leading to the outbreak of war in 1939 which was to have dramatic effect on the church.

Unconsciously in 1932, the vicar, through reference to past and present long service, portrays the working church in that small community. This could be seen as the last 'full dress parade', the last view of a church community which had a continuity with the long past. He thanks all those who help with the work of St. Michael's; the Church Wardens, Mr. Cook of Roydon Hall and Mr. Luck of Peckham Place; Colonel Potts, Treasurer and Secretary, of Little Roydon He thanks the Beadle, the Sexton, the Sidesmen, the Organist, the Choir, the Bell-ringers, the church cleaner, those who tend the churchyard, supply the altar with flowers, teach regularly in the Sunday School, the Secretary of the magazine, the Secretary of the Freewill Offering Fund. He found it most encouraging to have such a number of willing workers and to feel that they had such an interest in, and affection for, the old Parish Church.

Later in the year a special tribute was paid to the church cleaner whose love and affection for her church had been outstanding. She was no ordinary church cleaner. Mrs. Bishop who had died aged 87 had kept the church clean for 60 years. That work to her had been holy work. A golden link with the past had been broken.

Another long serving member was Mr. Waghorn the Beadle, who had been forced to resign because of illness and old age. He had held the office for 32 years. He had lived the whole of his 83 years within a mile or two of the church.

Also that year the vicar writes that the bell ringers led by their Captain Mr. Tom Saunders had recorded their historic achievement which is described in the Bells section.

It is not surprising that when the Archdeacon paid an official visit in 1934 he found that every thing connected with the church, its fabric, property, furniture, insurance, registers and plate was in good order. He was especially pleased with the cleanliness of the church and the care that was so obviously bestowed on it. Fortunately a photograph of the choir outing to Brighton remains as a memory of this happy time.

Less obvious to the eye was the vicar's spiritual work. When inviting members to one of the three Easter communion services he points out that *they are not coming to a service but to Him, a living Master and Friend who is only*

Figure 36. Choir outing to Brighton. 'Of course it was all made possible by the revolution caused everywhere by the all conquering motor coach, it is ugly but extremely useful'. Parish Magazine.

waiting for you to take the step and to give him the chance of pouring into your hearts and lives something of His very self'.

After five years the Rev Partridge exchanged livings with the Rev F.W. Bennitt Rector of Bletchley in Buckinghamshire who was in effect the last incumbent of the ancient church of St. Michael. His warm welcome he attributes to the affection the parishioners had for their last two vicars. However, although the parish is efficiently run he does not appear to have radiated affection. His son was a missionary to the Chinese in Singapore and he was himself interested in missionary work becoming an official of the Society for Promoting the Gospel and starting evening lantern lectures on missionary subjects. There is little of the personal touch in his monthly magazine message. He was a historian and his space was often composed of historical data of little interest to the majority of his small parish. The first mention of an impending crisis is March 1939 when he writes that:

> *'It is proposed to have some lectures on Air Raid Precautions in the school, they will be open to the public, both men and women. It is important to get familiar with the gas masks and also how to make a room proof against gas. A knowledge of these things should give us a feeling of confidence in these uncertain times'.*

This was followed by a series of lectures, First Aid Nursing in the Home, which were well attended but no other mention of war is made until the October issue when it is announced that October 1st has been fixed as a Day of Prayer in this time of war. However the crisis had already had it's effect because the children evacuated from Woolwich had arrived on September 1st with their own teachers. *'It will be very interesting for our own children to unite with them at school when their term begins on October 2nd.'* In the December issue he spoke about the neighbours who have received children into their homes.

'They threw their homes open and have shared their home life with their guests with loving care so that they have in fact become as one family. The children have quickly adapted themselves to being without their parents. The school is particularly happy.'

Those children made friendships which continue to this day! Nancy Folland was eight years old when she was evacuated from London to a completely different life style. Her separation from a loving family was made bearable because she and her sister were placed with the homely Bell family at Court Lodge and her life was centred on Court Lodge, the school and the church. She recalls that shortly before the services the church Beadle called at the cottage to change into his uniform which he kept there. This saved him from walking so far along the road wearing it. The gold trimmed, black jacket was carefully brushed and the black top hat which was made from a plush or velvet material was carefully smoothed round and round with a little handkerchief before he put it on. She recalls that the gentry sat in the pews at the front of the church, some more worshippers in the main part but *'most of us sat in the choir at the back'* and, from another recollection by a visitor, were watched over by the very firm Beadle!

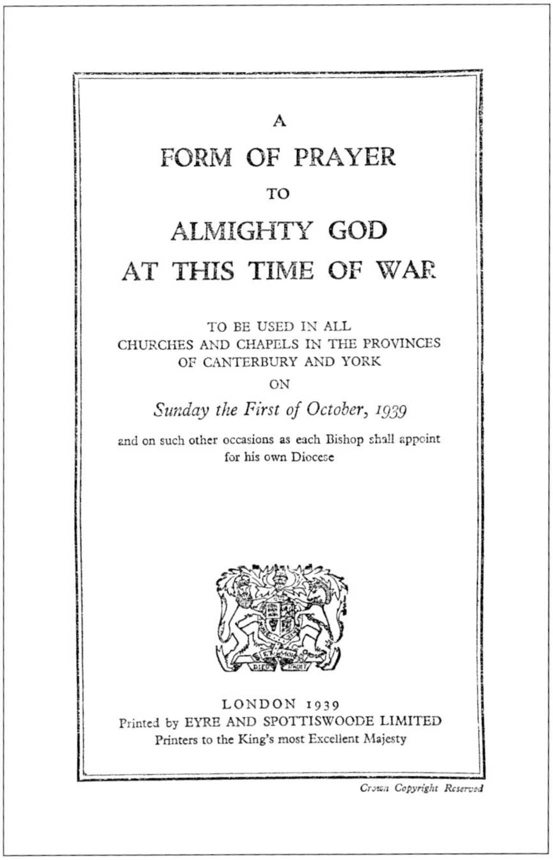

A

FORM OF PRAYER

TO

**ALMIGHTY GOD
AT THIS TIME OF WAR**

TO BE USED IN ALL
CHURCHES AND CHAPELS IN THE PROVINCES
OF CANTERBURY AND YORK
ON

Sunday the First of October, 1939

and on such other occasions as each Bishop shall appoint
for his own Diocese

LONDON 1939
Printed by EYRE AND SPOTTISWOODE LIMITED
Printers to the King's most Excellent Majesty

Crown Copyright Reserved

Figure 37. National Day of Prayer leaflet distributed to all churches.

Abruptly that issue of the October magazine informs that, *'I am proposing to bring the magazine to an end till happier times. We are told that there is a shortage of paper. I rather think the magazine is not so interesting now that we have exciting news of the war every day'.*

More things than the parish magazine were to come to an end. The prophetic words of 1932 were to be realised. *'The new year is bound to bring new conditions of living and fresh changes in our social life and what we have to do is first to understand them and then to face them, adapting ourselves to them with all the courage and wisdom that lie within our power'.*

The Second World War

Joan Bishop, a child, now Joan Walters, was in church the morning that war was declared. Mrs. Bennitt came to the door, she handed a note to William Bishop the Beadle who took it to the Rev. Bennitt. He announced from the pulpit that England was at war with Germany.

St. Michael's was at once affected by the war. Owing to the fact that many clergy were called to active service there was a reduced number available for parochial work and reorganisation was needed. As a result the Rev. Bennitt was returned to Bletchley and the church was cared for by the

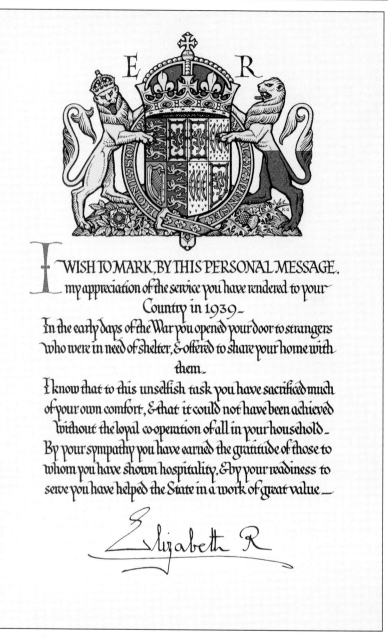

I WISH TO MARK, BY THIS PERSONAL MESSAGE, my appreciation of the service you have rendered to your Country in 1939.

In the early days of the War you opened your door to strangers who were in need of shelter, & offered to share your home with them.

I know that to this unselfish task you have sacrificed much of your own comfort, & that it could not have been achieved without the loyal co-operation of all in your household.

By your sympathy you have earned the gratitude of those to whom you have shown hospitality, & by your readiness to serve you have helped the State in a work of great value.

Elizabeth R

Figure 38. The Queen thanks those who had shared in the war effort by opening their homes to the evacuees.

vicar of Wateringbury and, of course, by the faithful churchwardens and congregation.

As in the first world war the Cook family of Roydon Hall were bereaved. Ralph Cook whose brother had been killed was to lose his two sons and see their names added to the war memorial.

Lieutenant John Hollingworth Roberts (formerly Cook) aged 36 of the Royal Naval Volunteer Reserve lost his life on the S. S Ceramic. The ship was a troop ship which left Liverpool on Monday 7th December 1942 carrying 378 passengers and 278 crew and gunners. It was torpedoed by U515 off the Azores on November 23rd. One survivor was taken out of the water by the U-boat for interrogation purposes. All others were lost. Lieutenant Roberts is commemorated on the Chatham Naval Memorial overlooking that town.[1]

Major Edwin Thomas Cook of the 6th Battalion Grenadier Guards lost his life on Monday 8th December 1943 and is buried in the Cassino Memorial Italy. He had taken part in the September Allied invasion of Italy which had the objective of drawing the German troops from the Russian front and from France where an offensive was planned for the following year.[2]

Also commemorated are:

William Burbridge who attended St. Michael's school.

A fellow school boy and living at Peckham Place, Sergeant Rear Gunner **Harold Stone** age 22 of the Royal Airforce Volunteer Reserve was in the crew of a Lancaster bomber when he lost his life on 13th June 1943. He is buried in the Reichswald Forest War Cemetery Germany. Although living in St. Michael's parish he is remembered on the Holy Trinity memorial.

The church fabric which had survived so many events during its long history was to be a victim of the war when on the 24th July 1944 a flying bomb exploded in the adjacent orchard behind the church and eighteen windows were blown. The roof received more serious damage. The school children remember that not only were they sent to pick up the glass but that they prided themselves that they picked up every piece! The windowless church caused problems as the Chairman of the Parochial Church Council, William Luck, explained to the War Damage Commission in December. He said that he had endeavoured to 'put back and stuff up' without success, that all the builders said they were 'on another damage' and could not undertake the work and that it was almost impossible to hold services in the church in the cold weather. He wondered if the committee could help in this matter. How long the church went windowless is not recorded but eventually in 1956 they were awarded £297 for stained glass and £541 for serious damage to the roof.[3]

WILLIAM BISHOP 1874-1962
Beadle of St Michael's 1930-1962
His love and faithfulness
were an inspiration to us all

Figure 39. The last Beadle. Mr. William Bishop was reported in the local press as being the last beadle in the country. His ancient duties included escorting the parish vicar before and after the service. His wand of office had been passed down through generations of past beadles.

References

1 The Commonwealth War Graves Commission Commemoration of Lt. Roberts, available on their website, stated that he had been serving on H.M.S. Euphrates. However Greenwich Maritime Museum found that this ship had long been out of commission. It was in fact a naval base in Basra, Iraq to which he was assigned. Mr. James Cook, a descendant, provided the information that the ship was a troop ship called the Ceramic which Greenwich traced in their records. On my pointing out this inaccuracy to the War Graves Commission the entry has been amended to show the cause of death 'lost in S.S. Ceramic'.

2 Commonwealth War Graves Commission.

3 C.K.S. War Damage Files DRb/RW284.

8. The End

After the war it was uneconomical to appoint a new minister for the ever dwindling population. Thus in 1947, a little over a hundred years since the division of the old parish into two separate parishes, a scheme was put into effect for their reunion into one parish and this was duly chronicled in the London Gazette.

The two benefices were to be *'permanently united together and form one benefice for the cure of souls under the style of the Benefice of East Peckham, and the parishes of the said benefice shall be united into one parish for ecclesiastical purposes. The parish church of the parish of East Peckham (St. Michael's) shall be the parish church. The Parsonage of Holy Trinity to be the residence of the united benefice'.* It was then that the St. Michael's vicarage lost its ancient relationship with the church and was sold for a private dwelling.

It was the changing post war conditions which caused the scheme to fail. No one could have foreseen that the scattered agricultural community would increase by over 1,000 and the number of houses by 454.

In the 1960s the planners determined to restrict a greatly increased population to new housing estates in the Pound area in order to conserve the rural aspect of the village. Whilst rightfully, and thankfully, preserving the natural beauty of the outlying areas it meant that St Michael's did not benefit from a new population and a congregation which might have

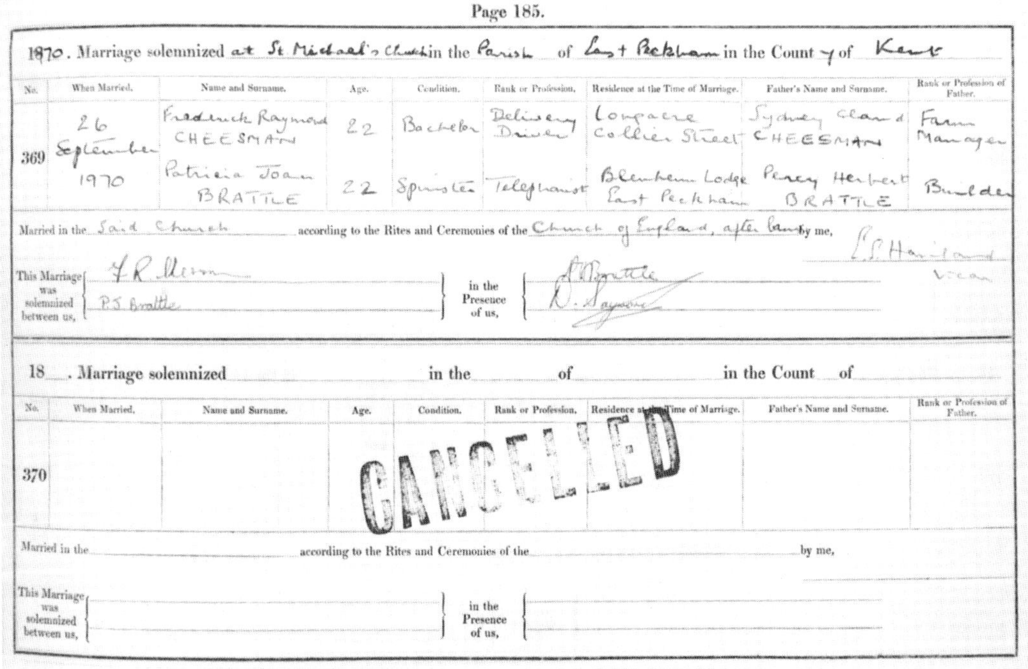

Page 185.

No.	When Married.	Name and Surname.	Age.	Condition.	Rank or Profession.	Residence at the Time of Marriage.	Father's Name and Surname.	Rank or Profession of Father.
369	26 September 1970	Frederick Raymond CHEESMAN	22	Bachelor	Delivery Driver	Longacre Collier Street	Sydney Claud CHEESMAN	Farm Manager
		Patricia Joan BRATTLE	22	Spinster	Telephonist	Blenheim Lodge East Peckham	Percy Herbert BRATTLE	Builder

1870. Marriage solemnized at St Michael's Church in the Parish of East Peckham in the County of Kent

Married in the *Said Church* according to the Rites and Ceremonies of the *Church of England, after Banns* by me, *P. P. Haviland* Vicar

This Marriage was solemnized between us, *F. R. Cheesman* / *P.J. Brattle* in the Presence of us, *A. Brattle* / *D. Seymour*

18___. Marriage solemnized _____ in the _____ of _____ in the Count ___ of _____

No.	When Married.	Name and Surname.	Age.	Condition.	Rank or Profession.	Residence at the Time of Marriage.	Father's Name and Surname.	Rank or Profession of Father.
370								

CANCELLED

Married in the _____ according to the Rites and Ceremonies of the _____ by me,

This Marriage was solemnized between us, in the Presence of us,

Figure 40. The last page of the marriage register – four hundred and twelve years since the first entry.

supported it financially. The problem of maintaining two churches in the parish reached its climax in 1969. The churchwardens met in November to discuss the great repairs which would have to be done at Holy Trinity in the near future and decided to open up discussions with the Diocese. The Diocesan surveyor replied quickly, estimating that £5000 would be needed to be spent on both churches in the next five years. As a result of this information the Parochial Church Council resolved that it must recommend that proceedings should be initiated to declare St. Michael's church pastorally redundant for the following reasons;

a) If Holy Trinity is not to suffer from lack of maintenance and improvement, St. Michael's cannot for much longer be maintained with the financial resources available and likely to be available in the state in which it is legally required to be maintained.

b) St. Michael's is so situated in the parish that it cannot so well fulfil the functions of a parish church as can Holy Trinity which is quite sufficient for the needs of the parish.

This was carried by sixteen in favour, none against, one abstention and four absentees.

The last service was a Harvest Festival on 1st October 1972 when thanks were offered for all those who had worshipped on this spot for over a thousand years.

The parish registers which had recorded the births, marriages and deaths of the common man for four hundred and fourteen years were closed. It was significant that the last bridegroom to be entered into the marriage register was Frederick Raymond Cheesman. The Cheesman family lived in the village and are recorded in manorial documents even before the registers were begun in 1558. The first baptism was entered in 1559 and between then and 1812 up to which point the registers have been indexed they were entered 437 times, and continued to be entered to the end. The bridegroom was a direct descendant of the family and it is fitting that the name should close this period of the church's history.

Equally fitting is the last entry in the burial register. Arthur Cook, the descendant of William Cook was buried on October 12th a few days after the official closure. William Cook had bought Roydon Hall from the Twysdens in 1837. The family came to love Roydon as much as the Twysdens had done and like them their joys and many sorrows were centred on St. Michael's. In 1938 Arthur Cook wrote 'A Manor Through Four Centuries', a history of Roydon Hall dedicating it to his father Ralph Montague Cook, 'in grateful tribute to his unvarying efforts to maintain Roydon and the traditions of its owners through these changing times'. The proceeds of the book were dedicated, even as the medieval Christians had requested in their wills, 'to the preservation of the fabric of St. Michael's church'. His death ended the 437 year association between the hall and the church.

PART II

9. The Exterior Building Stones

by B. C. Worssam (2000)

*T*he *building stands silent and mysterious and at first sight appears to be a heap of uncommunicative stone. When Dr. Bernard Worssam brought to bear his expertise as a geologist he gave the building a voice which spoke incisively through his description of the external building stone used in the church.*

The porch is 15th century, in Kentish Rag ashlar, all perhaps from one bed, of a pale rather yellowish grey colour. The doorway surround is of blocks from a bed of up to 12 inches thick with very fine mortar joints, much weathered, especially around the head of the doorway.

The South wall of the south aisle is of coursed rubble of Kentish Rag with some Tunbridge Wells sandstone; the quoins of its south east corner are of TWS ashlar. Three large Victorian Perpendicular windows (1857) and a similar one in the west wall of the south aisle are of oolitic limestone with calcite veins, almost certainly Bathstone. In the south wall the walling above the window heads is of squared blocks of Kentish Rag presumably rebuilt when the windows were inserted. A Kentish Rag buttress between the two more easterly of the three windows has ragstone ashlar quoins with pitted tooling and was probably built or rebuilt when the windows were inserted. Below the sill level of the windows the wall is rendered.

The South wall of the South chapel is of coursed rubble of Kentish Rag, has two large Perpendicular windows. These and a doorway beneath

Figure 41. The more pristine condition of the window figure heads is due to Victorian restoration.

the westerly one are of fresh looking Victorian Caen stone. The wall has two Kentish Rag buttresses with ashlar quoins.

At the South East corner of the South chapel a Kentish Rag buttress has some TWS quoin stones and the Kentish Rag east wall of the south chapel some TWS blocks. This wall and the east wall of the chancel (coursed rubble of Kentish Rag) each have a Perpendicular Bathstone and hence Victorian window. A buttress between the south chapel and the chancel is of carefully squared blocks of Kentish Rag with ragstone ashlar quoins with pitted tooling, so matching that on the south wall of the south aisle. The North east corner of the chancel is built of large side - alternate quoin stones of Kentish Rag from a bed of only six inches thick, set on end. The whole east wall looks later than the north wall and these quoins presumably date from the same time as the east wall.

The North wall of the chancel is mostly of only roughly coursed Kentish Rag rubble. Midway are two large squared-headed three light 15 or 16th century windows of Kentish Rag and at the west end of the wall a similar but single light

Figure 42. The Priest's door with figure heads. The door is now blocked for security reasons. The head on the left was stolen recently. Its return would be appreciated (Jessica Poynter).

Figure 43. Detail of the figure heads on either side of the Priest's door.

window in Bath stone, presumably a Victorian rebuild. High up near the east end of the wall is a small narrow round headed window, apparently with tufa jambs and head and presumably Norman, tufa being a favoured ashlar stone until worked out in about the mid 12th century (see Fig 44).

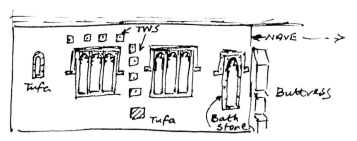

Some squared TWS blocks occur above the head of the more easterly of the three light windows while in the wall between this and the more westerly window are other TWS blocks, and at the foot of the wall one large squared block of tufa spaced out in a roughly vertical line as if they are a relic of a former quoin. If they are,

Figure 44. North wall structure.

this would imply that the eastern part of the wall including the round headed tufa window, is of a later date than the western part. These exceptional blocks apart, there seems to be no difference in type of stone or style of masonry throughout the north wall of the chancel, so on this evidence alone, if it were built in two phases there may not have been much of a time gap between them.

At the North East corner of the nave is a Kentish Rag buttress with ashlar quoins showing pitted tooling, so similar in style to the buttresses at the west end and on the south aside of the church, that it seems likely that all its buttresses are of Victorian build or rebuild. The north wall of the nave is cement rendered except for three square headed 15th century windows in much weathered Kentish Rag.

The Tower is also cement rendered, 'smothered in Roman cement' according to Newman 1980 (Buildings of England – West Kent and the Weald) who noticed the lancet high on its north side. There is a much weathered west doorway in large Kentish Rag blocks, pointed and wave-moulded, presumably 15th century.[1]

Terminology
Ashlar	Large stone blocks wrought to even faces and square edges.
Corbels	Block of stone projecting from a wall, supporting a horizontal feature.
Quoins	Dressed stone at the angle of a building.
Hood mould	Projecting moulding above an arch or a lintel to throw off water.
Abacus	Flat slab on top of a capital.
Ogee	Round headed arch.

Reference
1 The evidence for the date of the roman cement has now been found in the 1911 Vestry Book.

10. Architectural Appraisal

by Howard Jones (2001)

On entering the church the silence there is made eloquent by the expertise of architectural historian, Howard Jones, whose plans reveal the exciting development of the interior. This is supported by his century by century attribution.

The building comprises a chancel, nave, large south aisle, chapel and porch, a vestry on its north side and tower at the west end of the nave with a semi-engaged stair turret at its south corner, the whole surmounted by a small shingled spirelet. The roofs of the chancel and chapel were clad in Kent peg tiles. They were entirely re-roofed in 2003.

The Twelfth Century Church

Here the two disciplines, geology and architecture with independent voices agree on the evidence of the north wall of the chancel.

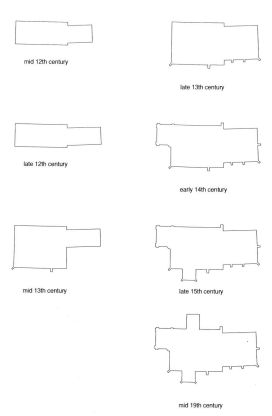

mid 12th century

late 13th century

late 12th century

early 14th century

mid 13th century

late 15th century

mid 19th century

Figure 45. St. Michael's Church. Development of Plan.
© Howard Jones

The earliest discernible masonry is in the western and central portions of the chancel north wall. At a point about three quarters of the way along to the east is a vertical row of stones, of tufa and Tunbridge Wells sandstone, and which do resemble quoin stones. If that is what they are, and they do not appear to be later insertions, they represent the original east end of the church, or the return for an apse. Tufa was most commonly used in Norman construction, but clearly subsequent to this is a remaining length of wall, which contains a late twelfth century Norman style window with dressings of tufa and that window is splayed internally without decoration. This cannot be very different in date from the earlier wall but the reason for extension or modification is not now clear.

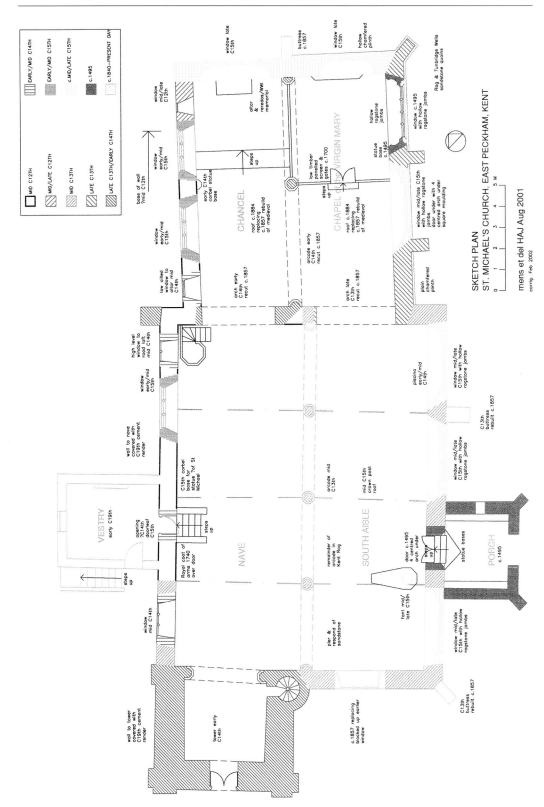

Figure 46. Plan of Church. © Howard Jones.

If the usual proportions of a Norman church were followed, the chancel was the size it is now, and the nave likewise, but with its west wall probably in line with the west walls to vestry and south porch, rather than in the present position. It is quite possible that the existing north and south doorways are in the location of their twelfth century predecessors.

The Thirteenth and Fourteenth Century Church

During the mid thirteenth century, if not the length it is today, the nave was extended westwards and the existing south aisle was formed. This has a four bay arcade on round piers with bell capitals and roll moulded bases typical of the Early English style, the pointed arches having a chamfer with a hollow chamfer moulding and a hood – mould over. All the capitals are slightly different, and the west respond and pier are of sandstone when the remainder is of Ragstone. The east respond was re-cut or re-built sometime in the nineteenth century. This aisle is almost as wide as the nave, but that it was built to its present width is suggested by the nature of the construction of its south wall, some of which is exposed within the later porch. The mortar is principally of clay with small chalk lumps and very little lime such as found particularly in the thirteenth century. The fact that this is not faced with closely packed flints, as outside beyond the porch, does suggest that a porch existed in this position in the thirteenth century.

Slightly later in the thirteenth century, **the south chapel** was added. The arch between it and the south aisles is supported on corbels, comprising a bell moulded cap on an inverted cone, semi-circular in cross section and terminating in a small roll moulded base semi-circular in plan. Apparent traces of red ochre survive. The arch it supports is of two orders of plain chamfers, without a hood mould. The outer one is continued past an extension of the cap to the corbel and terminates in a roll stop chamfer. All is of Early English style.

Later still, about 1300, **the chancel arch** was remodelled. It matches that between the south aisle and the chapel but is set on tapering semi-octagonal corbels. At about the same time a two bay arcade was formed between the chancel and the chapel. This has an octagonal pier and matching responds. The caps and bases to the piers, though apparently re-cut, surely reflect the original, and comprise smaller, alternate roll and angular mouldings under an abacus and surmounting a shallow hollow-roll with a half roll necking at its base, all redolent of the Decorated style. The general form of the arches to this arcade is similar to that in the nave, with a bolder, more undercut hood mould. The mouldings of the corbeled statue base match those corbels supporting the chancel arch so early fourteenth century. Though damaged the statue appears to be a woman and is most likely the Virgin Mary whose image usually stood in the chancel. The fact that it is not positioned centrally between the two fifteenth century windows provides evidence that it is of earlier date.

The **tower arch** is similar in form to the chancel arcade, so it and the tower presumably belong to the same period, as does a lancet high on the north side of the tower.

A little later in the fourteenth century, perhaps 1330, a square headed window with two ogeed and trefoil-headed lights was inserted at high level at the east end of the nave north wall. This was presumably to help illuminate the rood screen that would have spanned the chancel arch at the time. A similar, slightly larger window, was inserted into the west half of the nave wall. A few years later, a low cilled square headed cinque-foiled single light window with a dropped rere-arch was formed in the west end of the chancel north wall presumably to light an altar at that location.

Figure 47. The remains of a damaged medieval statue. Probably the Virgin Mary whose image usually stood in the chancel. © D Sampson.

Also some time around the early to mid fourteenth century the **nave north door way** was formed, possibly as a replacement for an earlier, Norman, one. It has a simple chamfered pointed arch with a raised segmental rere-arch internally. The five steps up to it are modern but there must have a medieval predecessor. The piscina at the east end of the south aisle south wall is also of this date.

The Fifteenth Century Church

In the early to mid fifteenth century, two windows were inserted in the chancel north wall, each of the three cinquefoiled lights with a flat head over all externally and a raised arch head internally, with plain splays. A similar window was inserted into the east half of nave north wall.

There was an extensive remodelling of the church later in the fifteenth century. The east walls of the chancel and south chapel were extensively rebuilt, the latter having a hollow chamfered plinth and a large pointed-arched three light window inserted in each. Both are in Perpendicular style: the two mullions are of through type with a quarter-ogee quatrefoil at the head in the centre light surmounting two reticulated lights with sub arcuated tracery to the top of the lights either side, each with an inverted dagger over a cinquefoil. Internally the splays are concave and their junction with the walls has a double ogee moulding. At the same time a window was inserted at the west end of the south wall of the chapel, and three into the south wall of the aisle. All are similar in form to those in the east wall but with simple reticulated tracery, and all have drafted margins. Three sets of mason's marks are visible. Although the tracery to all these windows was remodelled in the two nineteenth century restorations, it matches that shown in a painting dated 1807, (H. Petrie) so their form is likely to be the original. Two canopy tops in one window are all that survives of the original stained glass.

About this time also the priest's door to the south chancel of the chapel was added. It has a pointed arch and plain spandrel panels within a square frame, the hood mould to which originally terminated in figure heads, of which that to the west is missing.

The corbelled base to the east of the nave north door, possibly for a statue of St. Michael, and the surviving timber leaf to the nave north door, are both of the mid to late fifteenth century. The crown post trusses on moulded tie beams to nave and aisle roofs would appear to be contemporary also, as too the octagonal font which is set on a base not unlike a capital, with elongated hollow chamfered sides topped by a roll moulding.

A will dated 1495 records donations for the building of the **south porch** and the insertion of a window to the east end of the south wall of the chapel. The south door into the aisle was presumably part of this remodelling and comprises a pointed arch set within a concave moulded square frame, without a hood mould, with a blank quatrefoil and two mouchetts within each spandrel. The porch is four square, with diagonal stepped buttresses to the front corners, a small square headed two light window with plain heads to the east side, and a fine south doorway. This has a four centered arch over, supported off slender engaged shafts at the inner end of a concave splay with a heavily profiled mould over, and again, each sprandrel has a blank quarterfoil and two mouchetts.

About this date, a five light window was inserted in the east end of the wall of **the south chapel**. It comprises five cinquefoiled headed lights without tracery, under a very shallow four centred arch, with a hood moulding externally terminating in figure heads, and the internal splayed reveals concave with a double ogee vertical moulding each side.

The Later Church

Little is recorded or evident of changes to the architecture of the church during the sixteenth to eighteenth centuries but that which comes from documentary sources is recounted in the main text.

A **Vestry** of rendered brickwork was added off the nave early in the nineteenth century. It has a fireplace to the east, an arched window to the north, now blank but originally filled with a timber frame of gothic tracery, and a door to the west, accessed externally from above by a flight of stairs. This replaced an earlier building.

Two major episodes of work to the church are documented during the nineteenth century, the first under Joseph Clark 1857–1863 and Ewan Christian in 1883 which again are recounted from documentary sources in the main text.

In the first restoration, the roofs to chancel and south chapel were rebuilt in a much reduced, more classical style and pitch from the original and clad in slate. Sections drawn by Christian in 1883 show that these roofs had king post trusses with a flat plaster ceiling. The ungainly appearance of these new roofs was removed in 1883 when the roofs were returned to their former pitch, using scissor trusses boarded out below, and an internal battlemented cornice ornamented with paterae covering the wall plate.

11. Monuments

Monumental Brasses
by Philip Lawrence

In the central aisle just before the altar is a brass inscription in Latin to Richard Etclesley. Translated it reads:

> Here lies Richard Etclesley sometime rector of this church who died on the 20th day of the month of May in the year of our Lord 1426, upon whose soul may God have mercy. Amen.

This inscription is without accompanying effigy and the stone in which it is set contains no indent where such a figure could have been set. Yet Thorpe in his Custumal Roffensis written about 1760 shows a clear picture of the effigy set above the surviving inscription. This figure is of some interest.

Figure 48. The original monumental brass to Richard Etclesley, 1426, as illustrated by Thorpe in Custumal Roffensis 1760. Now only the inscription remains.

Thorpe shows him as a tonsured monk. The figure is not quite in the conventional mould of a priestly brass of the period. His full surplice is covered by a hooded almuce of fur and the apparent tassels are the tails of the animals whose fur is used. The long pendent ends of the almuce were a feature of the period. Regarded as being an indication of status the almuce was often used as a processional garment and worn under a cope. Here is an anomaly. Etclesley holds the chalice but he is not dressed as he would have been for officiating at Mass. In his will he left a gilt chalice to East Peckham church and desired to be buried in the chancel. Probably a monk, this rector might well have owed his appointment to the patronage of Christchurch Canterbury who had long held the manor.

A modest brass at the west end of the nave shows the figure of a man and woman in the dress of the early Tudor period. The inscription plate is lacking but a brass so similar in size, style and costume as to be indistinguishable can be found at Lindsell in Essex and is dated 1514.

William Cook in his Manor Through Four Centuries attributed the brass to William and Margaret Whetenhall 1539. Several factors suggest otherwise. Costume detail, in particular the lady's girdle, suggest a date earlier than 1539 when William Whetenhall died. An inexpensive brass like this, quite clearly an 'off the peg' product as witness its twin at Lindsell scarcely reflects the status of the Whetenhalls. Further, William

Whetenhall expressed the wish to be buried in the Lady Chapel next to his wife, who had predeceased him.

Then who are the neat figures still lying side by side nearly 500 years on? Possible candidates are William Cayser, dying in 1510 who asked to be buried in the body of the church 'prope matrem mea', and consequently his mother. Yet again the quality of the brass does not really express the status of the Caysers.

He is dressed in the standard civilian costume of the period.

He has hair almost to shoulders and a long gown trimmed at collar and front opening. His baggy sleeves also have cuffs with fur. A close fitting kirtle is visible at neck and wrists.

She wears the gabled head-dress of the early sixteenth century with the turned down collar, fur cuffs, girdle with three point fastening and pendant tasselled end.

In the south chapel, formerly the chancel of St. Mary, lies an intriguing outline. The indent of a brass to a man in armour contains but one or two surviving rivets. Nevertheless the outlines of both effigy and inscription are distinct. I tentatively date the figure on stylistic grounds as being of probable 1420–30 dating. A.G. Sadler in his survey of indents agrees with a date of 1420.

In any one period the number qualifying for an armigerous brass of this sort within a community like East Peckham must have been very limited.

Evidence from a will of the period offers the possibility of identifying the armoured figure. John Mew died in 1420 and in his will requested burial in the chancel of the Blessed Virgin Mary. Mew was a man of some substance called to attend the King and Council at Westminster in 1398 and was given permission in 1414 to celebrate mass in the private chapel of his home, known to have been the moated manor house of Albans, now Crowhurst Farm.[1 and 2] A Herald's Visitation of a later period shows the Mew family bearing arms. John is clearly of the date, locality and

Figure 49. Conversely, here the effigy remains but lacks the inscription. Who were these people? Brass Rubbing © Philip Lawrence.

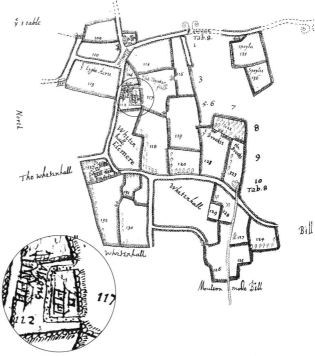

Figure 50. Twysden Estate Map 1632 shows the moated Albans Manor house, home of John Mew. It is now the site of Crowhurst Farm (Add Ms 34155 by permission of the British Library).

Figure 51. Neither the effigy nor the inscription remain but the surviving knightly outline suggests a date of 1420. © David Sampson.

Figure 52. The strange memorial to William Bansor. The inscription lacks a date. © C. Rainer.

status to have provided an appropriate identity for the long vanished brass

Historically fascinating if visually unattractive is the memorial situated midway in the aisle of the nave. A crudely made iron cross measuring 858 mm x 230 mm with a three stepped pedestal is set in a black stone. Below the cross a battered inscription plate of poor quality presents a challenge to the reader. It is a memorial to William Bansor.

William Bansor is first recorded as a rector before 1420 by Hasted who, it is believed, consulted the Twysden manuscripts in his recourse to local gentry for information. However detailed research has failed to find the source of this information. He is not recorded in the Archbishop's Registers but unfortunately that between 1327 and 1349, which might have recorded him, is missing.

The inscription is in English and appears to carry no obituary date. Bansor, having been assigned an early 14th century or early 15th century date this seems to be at odds with the attribution of a 16th century date to the inscription by Messrs Mill Stephenson and William Lack, both recognised authorities.

Several factors here are unique or puzzling: the absence of a date, the use of a brass inscription in combination with an iron cross, the use of English at so early a date and the mismatch of the reputed date of death with the type of plate.

I can think of one hypothesis which might account for this oddity. For this I have no evidence other than its plausibility.

The accession of Edward VI heralded a policy of destruction of symbols redolent of Rome. Among these general changes many brasses were destroyed. The fervent Queen Mary ordered a replacement of all Catholic iconography at the expense of the local congregation. Consequently economy was a major factor in the minds of church wardens. This scenario could explain a locally made iron cross, a cheap plate, the use of English, the mismatch of plate and obituary date. Even the absence of the date of death could have occurred because local people could not recall that date after the lapse of years. Have we here a shadow of the religious tension of the middle of the 16th century? Alternative explanations may become convincing if new evidence emerges.

Twysden Epitaph
by Geofrey Allibone

T he monument erected in 1689 remains in the church to this day. It was
inscribed in classical Latin and has recently been translated by Geoffrey
Allibone.

The remains of Sir Roger Twysden, Baronet, eldest son of Sir William Twysden, Baronet,
are placed here next to his father. He excelled in piety, prudence and other virtues no less
than in great and varied learning. He was very much engaged both in sacred and
secular learning, especially historical and the ancient monuments of our people. He also
suffered changing fortune. For, while in the time of King Charles the First in the
Parliamentary revolts he stood by his excellent King with the utmost constancy and

Figure 53. The Twysden Monument. © David Sampson.

loyalty, he suffered thereafter grievous hardships, harsh and lengthy imprisonment, and very great loss of his inheritance. But, with the kingdom regained by Charles the Second, after some years spent peacefully in his own house he suffered a stroke, and although he recovered from it, he was still never restored to his previous health, but, growing frail for seven months, at last approaching his 75th year, he changed this life for life eternal. He was born on 21st August, 1597 A.D., and died on 27th June, 1672 A.D.

He married Isabella, youngest daughter of Sir Nicholas Sanders in the County of Surrey, a woman endowed with a most excellent and saintly character. In order to care for her husband, so long oppressed and imprisoned, she suffered great hardships and misfortunes with rare patience and discretion. And finally, just as she lived piously, she also ended her life with the greatest piety on 11th March in 1656/7 A.D. according to the English reckoning, aged 52, and lies buried here next to her husband.

They were the parents of six children: William, the eldest, Baronet; Ann, wife (now widow) of John Porter, Esquire, of Lamberhurst in the County of Kent; Isabella; Frances, wife of Sir Peter Killigrew, Baronet, of Arwenack near Falmouth in the County of Cornwall; Roger, a young man of very great promise, who died on 20th February, 1676/7 A.D., and is here buried at the feet of his father; Charles.

In this Chapel rest the bodies of Sir William Twysden, Baronet, and Ann, his wife, both from Kent.

He, the eldest son of Roger Twysden, Esquire, of East Peckham was a man enriched with a wide range of learning, particularly accomplished in Mathematics, History, and Hebrew (especially the Holy Text). Famed for the prudence and honesty of his life, on 8th January, 1628, according to the English calendar, aged 63, in London at his own house he piously returned his devoted soul to God, and, buried in this ancient tomb of the Roydons and Twysdens on the 11th of the same month, he awaits the Saviour's trumpet.

But she, from the most noble family of the Finches of Eastwell in the County of Kent, in fact the eldest daughter of Sir Moyle Finch, Baronet, of Eastwell, and Elizabeth Heaneage, his wife, (who with a favour rare among our people, was made Viscountess of Maidstone by King James the First, then Countess of Winchelsea by Charles the First), was noted no less for her exceptional physical beauty than for her remarkable gifts of mind. She excelled in intellect, piety, generosity and charity. Death, which she expected when healthy and longed for when infirm, she met with a truly Christian resolution and piety on 14th November, 1638 A.D., aged 64.

She bore her husband seven children, all of whom survived her.

1. Roger, the eldest, mentioned in the adjoining tablet.
2. Elizabeth, wife of Sir Hugo Cholmeley, Baronet, of Whitby in the County of Yorkshire, died on 17th April, 1655, aged 55, and is buried here at the feet of her father.
3. Thomas, Knight and Baronet, one of the Judges on the King's Bench (as it is termed), the father of a large family by Jane, daughter of John Tomlinson, Esquire, died on 24th January 1682/3, aged 81, and lies buried at East Malling in the County of Kent.
4. Ann, wife of Sir Christopher Yelverton, Bart., of Easton in the County of Northamptonshire, died on 3rd December, 1670, aged 67, and is buried with her husband at the aforesaid Easton.
5. William died unmarried on 30th July, 1647, aged 36, and is buried in the Cathedral Church at Bath.
6. John lived unmarried and died on 13th September, 1688, aged 81 and four months, and lies buried in the parish church of Saint Margaret, Westminster.
7. Francis lived likewise unmarried and died on 6th April, 1675 A.D., aged 63, at East Malling, and in that same place has been entrusted to a tomb.

William Twysden, Baronet, son and heir of the aforesaid Sir Roger Twysden, Bart., placed this funerary monument for his grandfather at the bidding of his father, and himself for his father out of the respect owed to such a great parent, in the year of our Lord 1689.

The Royal Arms

Inside the church, on the north wall, though previously hung over the south door where the shadow can still be seen, are the Royal Coat of Arms dated 1740 when the King was George II. (1727–1760) When his father, George of Hanover had succeeded Queen Anne in 1714 the Royal Coat of Arms needed to be changed to include his other territories. The first three quarters remained unchanged; in the first quarter is England impaling Scotland, in the second is France, the third, Ireland, but the fourth quarter was divided into three; two golden lions on a red field for Brunswick, a blue lion on a gold background spattered with red hearts for Luneburg and in the lower part the white horse of Hanover on a red background galloping away from the lions. In the centre there is a small shield depicting the golden crown of Charlemagne. The accompanying illustration shows the details of the fourth quarter more clearly.

The supporters are the Lion for England and the Unicorn, a favourite emblem of Scottish history both introduced by James I. The

Figure 54. The Royal Arms. (For colour reproduction see page 127.)

motto 'Deiu and Mon Droit' (God and my right) the ancient English war cry was assumed as a regular motto by Henry VI (1422–1461). The shield is enclosed by the Order of the Garter with its motto *Honi soit qui mal y pense* and is surmounted by a sovereign's gold barred helmet facing the front. This is in turn surmounted by the crest which is a crown on which stands a splendid lion who himself wears a crown. The crest is a figure or device which was originally attached to the knight's helmet so he could be easily distinguished in battle. Round the shield is the mantle which is based on the small garment hanging from the knight's helmet to protect him from the sun.

References

1   Close Rolls 1396–99.
2   British Library Ms. 34,155 Twysden Estate Maps.

Figure 55. Sketch illustrating the detail of the fourth quarter of the Royal Coat of Arms.

12. Victorian Stained Glass

Acknowledgements to Peter Cormack, William Morris Gallery.

The quality of the stained glass has escaped due recognition. All artists involved with St. Michael's were of the highest reputation having all been associated with and influenced by the work of Pugin the Gothic revivalist architect.

William Cook 1852 (the younger). On the south wall of the small chancel. Identified by Peter Cormack of the William Morris Gallery as the work of the Irish artist Michael O'Connor. (1801–67). It depicts praying/worshipping angels in the tracery lights. The now empty three lights originally depicted full size angels. The window was damaged by bomb blast in the Second World War and the fragments were collected by school children. This is the first of the Cook memorials. East Peckham owes a great debt to him. He was a pioneer of education, founding St. Michael's school about 1835 under the auspices of The Home and Colonial Infant School Society which was the pioneer of infant education in England. In his will he left money for its continuance and money also for the building of a new school in the Trinity Parish providing it was built within 21 years of his death. (The present village school). His stipulation was *'providing that the Holy Scriptures be read to the children for half an hour each day and explained in their presence by a. trained teacher'.*

Figure 56. The Praying Angels. Repaired after war damage. Memorial window to William Cook (the younger).

Education has long since broken faith with these pioneers (see Margaret Lawrence, 'Peckham Pupils. The Development of Education in a Kentish Village').[1]

Thomas Hugh Boorman. This was no doubt one of the windows destroyed by the bomb in the Second World War. It was probably in a window on the north wall of the chancel as his family were tenants at Parsonage Farm, (Little Roydon) which still carried the responsibility for the chancel. It was reported by the Kentish Journal as the work of Warrington who was described as an 'Artist in Stained Glass, Heraldic and Decorative

Painter'. (1796–1869) Thomas Hugh Boorman came from Sussex to Branbridge Mill as a stone dresser at the age of 13 and married Margaret Martyr the miller's daughter ten years later in 1794. He died in May 1859 aged 90 and had requested to be buried in the family vault which lies to the west of the church porch. It was he who altered the history of East Peckham by stipulating in 1841 that Holy Trinity should be a separate parish and supplied the money to provide for a minister to Holy Trinity.[2] He also founded the Boorman Trust in 1840 which provided alms houses for his retired bargemen from the Medway Navigation Company. The building in Snoll Hatch Road is administered by the Boorman Alms Houses Trust.[3]

Figure 57. The memorial window to William Cook (the elder). The Nativity, the Crucifixion and the Resurrection.

Mary Anne Cook. The east window of the small chancel. The three light window depicting the Ascension is reported by the Kentish Journal and confirmed by Peter Cormack as the work of John Hardman and Co. He also points out some later repairs and restoration no doubt as a result of bomb damage. The damage may account for the fact that the dedication is missing. Hardman, a Roman Catholic had been directly supervised by Pugin and was concerned with new ways of approaching stained glass. The window was given by William Cook in memory of his wife who died in 1862 as reported by the Kentish Journal.

Figure 58. The South View of Roydon Hall. The home which the Cook family cherished for its long history. (By permission from the Spiritual Regeneration Movement of Great Britain)

William Cook (the elder). The chancel east window glass given by the Archdeacon in 1863 seems to have been replaced by the magnificent Cook memorial window of 1869. This has been identified by Peter Cormack as also the work of John Hardman and Co. Its three lights depict the Nativity, the Crucifixion and the Resurrection. It was no doubt bomb damaged and has been repaired/restored in parts e.g. the figure of Christ in the central light. The dedication is:

> *'In memory of William Cook who died in the faith of Christ crucified April 19th 1869 age 85 years'.*

William Cook born 1784 was the founder of the Cook family of Roydon Hall. His full story is recounted by his descendant in A Manor Through Four Centuries. As a young man of 21 years he left his North Norfolk farming home and family and went to London to seek his fortune. With little education his application to be a clerk at the bank of Overend and Gurney (of Norfolk association) failed on account of his poor handwriting. In retrospect this was fortunate because he became apprenticed to a London merchant where his qualities of hard work, punctuality and good behaviour so impressed his employer that they later became partners. William's success expanded until he eventually conducted his business at 22 St. Paul's Churchyard where the family were to trade for over a hundred years. It was said to be *'a business upon which hung the commercial welfare of thousands of shoppers and traders throughout the Kingdom and Empire'*. At an early date he became a member of the Livery of the Worshipful Company of Drapers and took an active part in civil life and administration. This he continued in his new life in East Peckham when he bought Roydon Hall from the Twysdens in 1837. He was a most generous benefactor whom other members of his family were to emulate.

The Rev Middleton Onslow. Placed in the Norman window, on the north wall of the chancel and depicts the Good Shepherd. Identified by Peter Cormack as the work of Clayton and Bell, the well known London firm. The style suggests that George Daniels may have drawn the cartoon. He was for many years the firm's principal figure draughtsman. No sign of war damage is apparent and it may be that the window was protected by the deep window embrasure and small size of the window.

Dedication on a brass memorial plate is *'To the glory of God and in loving memory of Middleton Onslow for 30 years vicar of this parish'*.

References

1   See Margaret Lawrence. Peckham Pupils.
2   See Margaret Lawrence. The New Church.
3   CKS U1163 T5 Bundle B 1840.

13. The Churchyard

The churchyard is both an art gallery and a library with the pictures and the words having many stories to tell.

The original yard was approximately one and a quarter acres, larger than the usual area designated as God's acre. There were and still are four entrances. Originally church yards were not enclosed by boundary walls. Unfortunately because of the loss of the Shoreham Deanery records there are no early Bishop's Visitation records which might have given information, as some records do, as to when the wall was built and of its' further maintenance. However evidence is concealed in the tithe dispute of 1671. Sir Roger Twysden, born 1597, and his brother Judge Thomas Twisden, born 1602, and *'many other ancient men could remember a small tenement wherein one Crowhurst lived adjoining the churchyard wall'*. This gives a probable date of 1610 for boyhood memories while the tenement adjoining the wall supports an earlier date for the wall's existence.[1]

It was reported in the Vestry book on many occasions that the wall was broken down and in need of repair but it was not until 1914 that a solution to the problem was found. The eastern wall was removed in order to embrace the churchyard extension of just over a third of an acre, making a new total area of over one and a half acres. The stone which was suitable for salvage was used to repair the remaining walls. It was found that the walls had no foundations and that they were resting on the natural rock below.

The boundary of the old eastern wall is marked by a bank and by a portion of wall retained because of an inserted plaque. The Rev. Ryley, writing in 1914, records that letters had at sometime been cut on the plaque, intimating that they were at that date no longer legible. It is thought that the plaque relates to the entry in the parish register for 1669 stating:

'J D excommunicated, was buryd under the wall without ye churchyard betwixt the gate and the walnut tree.'

JD is certainly John Day, the Anabaptist excommunicated in the Churchwardens' Presentments on several occasions for failing to conform to the requirements of church attendance. Consequently he was refused burial in the churchyard. A new wall extended by thirty yards in 1926 formed a new boundary to the south east of the new burial ground. The cost of the stone and its cartage from Nettlestead quarry was borne by Mr. Cook of Roydon Hall.

Surviving records of wall repair show that it was the responsibility of the parishioners to keep it in repair and they are of interest to those who study stone work. The eastern wall of 1926 is in contrast to the wall to the west of the lych gate which embodies a remnant of early stone work carved with a fleur de lisle. A walk around the wall observing the various methods of stone laying and the size of the stones will reveal work of various dates.

Figure 59. Isaac Honey 1695. A surviving early stone. Isaac lead 'an honest and sober life'.

The Art Gallery – Headstones

Here lie buried the centuries of East Peckham's population. Burial in the churchyard was normal except for the elite who in earlier times were buried in the church in the hope that the fact of lying nearer the Mass would assist their journey through Purgatory. The first remaining mention of churchyard burial is that of Richard Peckerill who in his will of 1450 requested that he might be buried in the churchyard of East Peckham. Thereafter as more wills survive for the period this becomes a standard request, but all evidence of burial has vanished. There was one memorial for all – the churchyard cross still to be seen in many churchyards. If other memorials existed they were most likely made of wood which deteriorated and, as time and space demanded, burials took place over previous sites. This practice left no evidence of date or identity. There is certainly nothing to record the 83 burials when East Peckham, in particular, was devastated by the influenza outbreak of 1558–1559. This number was five times the average yearly burials in the 1560s.

Headstones became fashionable following the constraints of the Commonwealth. That the yard at St. Michael's would have displayed such stones is suggested by the yeoman status of the indigenous families whose members died at this period, such as, the Stanfords, the Martins, the Cheesmans and Pattendens and by the fact that a representative group of seven unusually early stones have been recorded in recent years. The sunken stumps around the yard suggests that there had been many more.

Earliest evidence is the headstone of John Smith who died in 1656. Of the same year is the headstone to Catherine, wife of Henry Godfrey who died 2nd January 1656. Catherine would have known the wife of Thomas Somner whose early death was in 1645 at 22 years of age. Her name and those of her two children in 1645 and 1651 at 13 and 11 years were recorded later on her husband's stone when he died in 1675 aged 63 years. Thomas Gardener, by his will recorded as a bricklayer, had a headstone dated 1676.[2]

Thomas Hatch Senior who died 1682 aged 75 years and his wife who died 1680 aged 72 years had headstones as does Thomas Castleden

Figure 60. The sand in the hour glass on the grave of Ann, wife of John Martin, symbolises the end of life's time. This was one of the 'fashionable' death and mortality themes. Photo Rev. Bennet, pre 1939.

Figure 61. Another death and mortality theme – a 'barbaric death mask' on the grave of Anne Biggenden. Photo Rev. Bennet, pre 1939.

who died 1689 aged 69 years. Isaac Honey who *'led a sober and honest life and made a good and pious end'* in 1695 at the age of 53 complete this group of unusually early headstones. Isaac was principally concerned for his soul and had no concern for his body leaving it to his executors to bury him in Christian burial. Their tribute to him has endured for more than three hundred years.[3]

Figure 62. A later more triumphant approach to death, the angels sound trumpets of welcome. Photo Rev. Bennet, pre 1939.

These headstones are characteristic of the period being small, thick, and with lettering boldly cut and with no decoration. It is thought that their survival is due to the Rev. F.W. Bennitt (incumbent 1934–1939). With a prescient awareness, at that date, he wrote in the parish magazine that the old headstones in the churchyard were of great interest but unfortunately they were decaying through exposure to wet and frost. He said that lichen and moss retained the wet and then the frost did the damage. He had the stones cleaned and with foresight photographed 36 of them 'so as to preserve a record' and some of these photographs have been found. He was also influenced by the work of F. Burgess whose book Monumental Inscriptions was published in 1963 after 25 years research and remains the classic work on the subject.

Mr. Burgess visited St. Michael's churchyard in the early days of his research and commented that *'it was a typical churchyard in which to study the ornament and imagery used by Kentish gravestone carvers'.*

It was indeed an art gallery portraying an imagery of restoration faith replacing that of the medieval period. Frequently displayed is the death and mortality theme illustrated by the hour glass, death masks, which are barbaric in appearance, and skull and cross bones, often giving rise to mistaken thoughts of pirates' graves.

This theme develops with the circular serpent engulfing its own tail representing eternity and the urn depicting the place where the bones were kept. Angels lend a more triumphant note symbolising the presence of heaven and those blowing trumpets proclaim victory over death with the resurrection. Flowers and trees were also used.

During the last half of the 18th century biblical scenes became popular on gravestones and St. Michael's

Figure 63. An example of crossbones. Photo Rev. Bennet, pre 1939.

Figure 64. The Good Samaritan. The high quality workmanship for William Martin's grave 1781. The characters are dressed in contemporary style clothing. Picture from F. Burgess, Monument Inscriptions.

had three superb examples. The earliest is Ann Long 1779, who lived at Pimms Place Bush Road (previously called Long's). Here the Agony in the Garden of Gethsemane was depicted. The central group was flanked by Christ holding a cross. There was a mourning attendant and the background of Jerusalem. This picture could be seen until recently but now only the Rev. Bennitt's photograph remains for a record (not reproduced).

That of William Martin 1781, who belonged to the Addlestead Farm family (Tonbridge Road), was of such quality that it was illustrated in Mr. Burgess' book. The background of domed, spired and castelated buildings is meant to represent Jerusalem. The Samaritan is dressed in contemporary style clothing – feathered bonnet, doublet and trunk-hose. He is pouring oil into the wounded man's arm. The Samaritan's horse is tethered behind him. To the right amid trees stands a robber, dressed like a Georgian farmer and carrying a cudgel. The Levite is dressed in clerical garb. There is the command *'Go and do likewise'*.

The Good Samaritan is also depicted on the stone to John Sully 1784. The picture may also refer to the incident when angels ministered to Christ after the temptation in the wilderness, an apposite comparison to the parable.

Supreme in artistry and extravagance is that of John Stanford who died in 1792 aged 38. Against a background of tasselled drapes every item of popular funerary expression is portrayed; the skull, the serpent, the urn, the angels, the book of life and a palm tree signifying victory over death. The picture was fortunately taken by Rev. Bennitt. Sadly little remains today of the carving.

Unfortunately the stones have further deteriorated in the years since Burgess' visit but the inscriptions were recorded in 1965 by two schoolgirls and again in 1985 by the Maidstone group of the West Kent Family History Society who included those inside the church. A total of 429 inscriptions were recorded of which 325 relate to burials in the original churchyard.[4]

Churchyard gravestones based on first surname on headstone

1650–1700	1700–1750	1750–1800	1800–1850	1850–1914	undated
7	57	59	109	52	41

The increased population which had caused problems with church seating accommodation in 1835 also placed pressure on burial space. The area south of the church shows the graves to be tightly packed. The pressure on space meant that sites had to be re-used with only a shallow depth and there were reports that bones from previous burials were sticking out of the ground. By 1883 the problem was acute and the Vestry considered the necessity of closing the burial ground and finding other ground. There was room on the north side but they said it was useless by reason of solid rock within a few feet of the surface. It was not until 1911 that the Rural Dean supported the urgent need for enlargement of the churchyard. Arrangements were made with Lord Falmouth to exchange a piece of land to the east of the yard for a similar amount of glebe land north of the vicarage.

Plots could not be bought since no one owned the churchyard but those who could afford it strengthened their family graves in order to prevent their future disturbance and reuse.

The most obvious way to secure a site was to surround it by railings. The most prestigious is that of the Boorman/Marytr family. It is on a raised slab situated next to the church porch. Because of its quality it has Listed status. To the east is the fenced Biggenden tomb, the only one which had an entrance vault. Nearby are the substantial rails of the Martyr graves. Another method of securing a site is illustrated by the raised table tomb recording John Mason who was a doctor in the village for 60 years and the Luck's box tomb raised on a slab. Both are to found just inside the lych gate. Other means of securing a site were by the use of curbs and stones. The large flat stone outside the church door is thought to have been a coffin rest.

Figure 65. The supreme example of funerary expression. John Stanford's family ensures that every item is displayed. Fortunately the example is preserved by the Rev. Bennets' camera, pre 1939, but little can be seen today.

The Library – Epitaphs

Of the 325 recorded headstone inscriptions only 35 include an epitaph in addition to the genealogical details. Those up to the end of the 18th century are concerned with mortality and death. The ubiquitous lines 'As I am now so shall you, Therefore prepare to follow me', has a more sophisticated version on the stone of Thomas Austen 1715:

Stand still reader and shed a tear
Upon the dust that
Slumbereth here
And when you have
Read the state of me
Think on the glass that runneth for thee.

Most are sentimentally worded, as expressed by Elizabeth wife of William Fordham who died 1827 age 33 years:

Oh husband dear my life is passed
Love to each other while it did last
And now for me no sorrow take
But love my children for my sake.

It has been observed that in general there is a marked absence of any Christian statement of faith on headstones until the end of the 18th century when use is made of short biblical texts indicating belief in salvation through faith. However there are no such examples here, but as 42 stones are unreadable and more have vanished completely, there is the possibility that they existed.

The first recorded expression of faith is that of Thomas Ellis 1798 aged 38 years:

Here buried in the hope of joyful resurrection.
My flesh shall slumber in the ground
Till the trumpets joyful sound
Then burst the tomb with sweet surprise
And in my saviour's image rise.

Similarly expressive and individual (incidentally illustrating the practices of ignoring lineage and punctuation), was that of John Cripps 1802 aged 77. His wife had died many years before in 1747 aged 29 years:

Mourn not my bosom friend dry up your weeping
eyes my body only in this grave it lives my souls
I hope unto a better place is flown where it will
wear an everlasting crown so should you
rather rejoice at the sight of death but pray
for both our heavenly repose for what God
giveth he can take and when he will new
gift can make therefore my friend I pray sit
calmly down and rest contented all they change
doth come and after they mortal life I hope
we both shall be then with our blessed Christ
by much greater love and felicity.

An example of the statements of faith by the Methodist Welfear family is that of Emily aged 30 who died 1876:

Let not your heart be troubled neither let it be afraid
For I shine in the light of God
His likeness stamps my brow.
Through the shadow of death my feet have trod
And I reign in the glory now.

The Library

The churchyard is a library in which the only category is non fiction. Each person buried has a unique story but only a few can be recounted.

The tomb of *'John Mason who practised as a surgeon for upwards of 60 years'* and that of his wife *'Mary Westbrook Mason, daughter of William Fleet'*, which stands to the left of the lych gate, conceals a strange story because some of the inscription has faded since it was recorded by the schoolgirls in 1965. It then recorded:

'Within this vault (by permission of her aunt, Mrs. Mason,) are deposited the remains of Mary Fleet Mitchell of Charles Street, Cavendish, widow of the late Rev. George Henry St. John Mitchell for many years curate of this parish. She was the daughter of Thomas and Martha Hill Andrews and died January 3rd 1836 age 61 years'.

Her mother Martha was another daughter of William Fleet of East Peckham and sister of Mary Westbrook Mason. They both benefitted from the will of their father in 1790, a very wealthy man, as did his granddaughter who became the heiress of a considerable fortune. So much so that a trust was set up for its management. The preamble to the document refers to *'Mary Fleet Mitchell the wife of the Rev. St. John Mitchell now approaching her sixteenth birthday'*![5]

At that time the Rev. Mitchell was 28 years old. Canon Ryley writing in the parish magazine in 1929, claims that the curate ran away with the girl, married her, sought forgiveness, got it and came back to East Peckham, but unfortunately does not give his source of information. How much was her husband influenced by the young lady's fortune? To his credit when he died intestate his personal estate was only worth under £300.[2] Consoled by her three daughters his wife erected a monument high up over the arches in the south aisle:

> *'Near this place are deposited the remains of the Rev. George Henley St. John Mitchell B.A 27 years curate of this parish, 13 minister of Leeds with Broomfield in this county who while performing divine service in this church on the General Thanksgiving Day Jan 13th 1814 was suddenly attacked with apoplexy and died in a few hours in the 52 year of his age.*
> *He was the eldest son of Thomas Mitchell Esq of Ballyrom in Ireland and Alice his wife the granddaughter of Sir Robert Echlin. Bart. of Rush House in the County of Dublin. This tablet is erected in his memory by his bereaved widow'.*

Unfortunately Irish National Archives have no record of him.

This story has consequences to this day because his daughter Miss Elizabeth Anne Mitchell dying in 1885 bequeathed £50 in Consuls, *'the interest to be distributed at the vicar's discretion in bread and meat among the poor'*. This remains a Church charity administered by Holy Trinity Church![6]

The memorial to Richard Stanford, to the east of the church, now scarcely readable, is a special story for the history of the village. It reads:

> *'Sacred to the memory of a man who is deeply mourned as he was highly valued for his many excellencies – Richard Stanford Esq. After long and severe suffering borne with the fortitude and submission that only religion can supply left this world of sorrow for a happier clime and brighter skies on the 10 June 1836 in the 47th year of his age. His closing scene exemplified the declaration of the writ that the righteous hath holpen the earth. With him terminated the male branch on their own land in this parish for a period of more than three centuries.'*

In fact the Stanford name is first recorded in the parish in 1169 and continued to be found in documents even before the parish registers begin to record their name making overall a total of 667 years.[7] The sad twist to the story is that the Stanford blood continued. John Stanford his father, buried beside him, not marrying till he was 35 years old, had a relationship which produced an illegitimate

Figure 66. The tragic memorial for James Grey, gamekeeper.

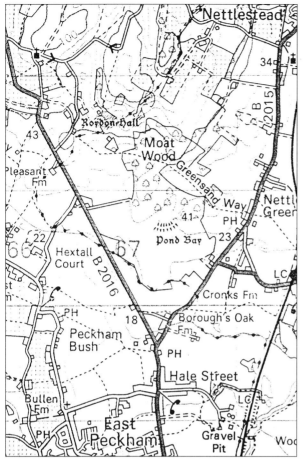

Figure 67. Moat Wood where the murder of James Grey took place. Map before by-pass. (Courtesy of Ordnance Survey.)

son and daughter to whom he gave his name and made provision for John Stanford Fordham and his sister in his will. Over the centuries the Stanford family lived in various village farmhouses but their early settlement seems to have been in the Goose Green area where the main road, the A26 was known as Stanford Street in manorial documents of 1566.[8] His inscription also represents the Weslyean movement in East Peckham because Richard's widowed mother was one of the original Methodists who signed the application for a license.

Richard was active in the work of that church in 1810, holding cottage meetings. In establishing Methodism in the village the Stanfords contributed much to the universal church in East Peckham.

Sadly and recently broken is the memorial to James Grey:

*'To the memory of James Grey
gamekeeper at Roydon Hall
who was shot by poachers on January
22nd 1862 aged 39 years.
'man cometh forth like a flower and is cut
down. Job 4 verse 2'.'*

For the previous three years the Roydon Hall estate, owned by Mr. Cook, had been under the management of James Gray. He had been born on the renowned Felbrigge estate in Norfolk where his duties as a gamekeeper had dated from his boyhood. He was a fine, tall, strapping fellow in the very prime of life and with a degree of personal courage which made him shrink from no danger in the performance of his duty. He lived in Rook Lodge on the Roydon Hall estate in the parish of Nettlestead, just south of the junction of Martins Lane and Seven Mile Lane. In the early morning of January 22nd, between 12 and 1 a.m he was awakened by an under keeper and a watcher who had heard the firing of guns in Moat Wood which contained the feeding place for the game. Although they were off duty three other watchers who had heard the shots joined Gray in looking for the poachers. The six men armed only with bludgeons, found themselves confronted by a gang of eight poachers, seven of whom were armed with guns. They had completed their work of slaughter and were just leaving the wood with their spoil. On the keepers making their appearance the leader of the poachers ordered, *'Form in a line and shoot the first man who comes near'*. Undaunted by this Gray advanced confidently towards them saying, *'Surely you are not such cowards as to fire at unarmed men'*. He had scarcely spoken the words when one of the gang fired his piece, the contents lodging in the keeper's left thigh. Although very severely wounded, Gray made a dash at the fellows, two of whom he knocked down with his life preserver, and other keepers coming to his rescue a general fight ensued, the poachers using the butts ends of their guns, in the course of which Gray received a severe blow upon the temple and, already exhausted by the loss of blood which flowed fast from his thigh, he fell to the ground. At this point the poachers made off. By this time Gray was fast sinking and asked to be taken home so that he might see his wife before he died. A delay of some time occurred while a gate was found to carry him and a doctor to be called. Mr. Biggenden, Surgeon, of East Peckham, later said that all efforts to save his life were ineffective. He remained conscious to the moment of his death at 5 am.

At the inquest held at Roydon Hall the surgeon said that the whole charge had entered the thigh and the bleeding was very great and he died from exhaustion and shock to the system. The Coroner accepted that evidence and recorded *'that by whom the gun was discharged there is no evidence to show'*.

On the following Monday six local men were remanded by the magistrates on suspicion of being concerned in the poaching affray but the following week they were released when it was shown that there was no evidence to be brought against them. Gray had maintained that he recognised the men as being 'the Malling gang' but in spite of Mr. Cook contributing to the award of £100 no one came forward with any information.[6]

The widow was left to support five children. She gave birth to a sixth a few days later.

A more recent and happier story is that of Dr. Black *'who lies in the shadow of St. Michael's looking down over the country in which so many years of his busy life were spent and over the people in whose hearts he still lives'*. The Rev. Ryley, in November 1932, wrote on behalf of the whole village recalling his great kindness of heart and sympathetic outlook, a friend of everyone as well as being their doctor for thirty years. He had been Secretary of the War Memorial Committee and under his guidance the Holy Trinity war memorial was erected. He was also instrumental in establishing the Red Triangle Hut in The Freehold to help those who returned from the war with mental and physical injuries. He had remained an enthusiastic trustee of the Hut as well as being a supporter of every social activity. His wife, much of the same nature, had collected the money to built a nurse's house in 1928 to house a village nurse. They had been presented with an album containing an illuminated address and the names of 800 people on the occasion of their Silver Wedding. This remains with added

Figure 68. Dr Black, village doctor for thirty years, secretary of the Holy Trinity War Memorial Committee, founder and life trustee of the Red Triangle hut. Buried at St. Michael's

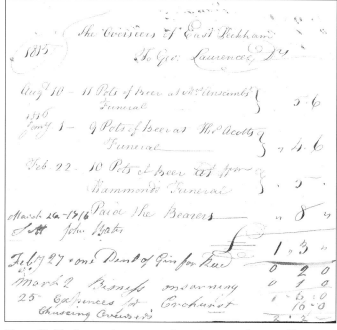

Figure 69. The Overseers' payment to George Lawrence for pots of beer at paupers' funerals.

newspaper cuttings and photographs. What distinguished him above all was his Christian faith.

Many people pursuing their genealogy will find their forebears in the parish burial register but will seek in vain for a headstone in the graveyard. A headstone is to some extent a status symbol, implying the family's economic ability to provide for a burial enhanced by the memorial. But there were a vast number of the unemployed, sick, destitute and widows who relied on parish support not only for earthly existence but after their death. Some records of burial lie in the undertaker's bills presented to the Overseers for payment. Among them:

Expenses on account of the parish of East Peckham by John Ashton

1815	April 9th Paid Mr. Lawrence for a pint of gin for the women attending	
	Dame Crayford at her death	2s.0d
	April 16th Paid men one shilling for carrying her to the grave	8s.0d
	Paid Mr. Lawrence for 10 pots of beer for the men, the clerk and myself	
		5s.0d
	May 7th Paid 8 men 1s each carrying Ann Waterman to the grave.	
	10 potts	

1816	Coffin for Master Martin	£1.4s
	Parsons fee	3s
	Clerks fee	6s
	William Homewood	10s

Children were equally cared for;

1823	6 boys carrying Fanny Hodge to the ground	3s (and no beer money!)
	Coffin for a child unknown	7s
	To the burial of it	6s

For some reason the 'baeueral' of J Rofe and the 'beuearel' of George Morris cost only 13s in each case.

Funeral Customs

The tradition was for bodies to be wrapped in a shroud of linen for burial but in 1666 Charles II decreed that in future all dead bodies should be buried in a woollen shroud in order to stimulate the declining wool trade. Those who refused to comply were obliged to pay a fine for the use of the poor of the parish. Perhaps Arthur Cheesman of Snoll Hatch had this in mind when he requested in 1667 that he be buried with no more expense than befits a poor man. The burial of Isabella Twysden in 1681 was the first to be noted in the parish register as *'buried in linen'*. The entries are useful because they indicate the financial status of the families.

People continued to give alms to the poor as had been the practice in the medieval period. Among them, Alice Stanford aged 92, making her will in 1643, devised three bushels of wheat to be given to the poor on the day of her funeral as well as 20 shillings.[9] Her descendant John, in 1752, left his clothes to the poor, *'the minister and churchwardens to distribute such clothing to and among the poorer inhabitants'*.[10]

Families liked to be buried together. Richard Stanford

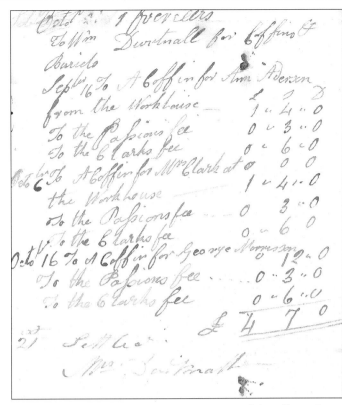

Figure 70. The Overseers' payment to William Dartnall for coffins and expenses for paupers' funerals

1629[11] and Edward Martin 1695[12] both wished to be buried near their relations while Arthur Cheesman was more specific in that he wished *'to be buried nigh unto my father and brothers with whom and all the faithful Christians I assure myself to rise at the last day'*.

Sarah Hodge, 1728, is one who took a particular interest in arranging her funeral. *'I desire to be buried at the parish church of East Peckham near where my husband was interred for whom and myself I have a set up a double headed gravespiece. I desire to be buried in linen and to have a sermon preached at my funeral in like manner as my husband was buried'*.[13]

Mary Featherstone, 1778, wished gloves to be given to all those who attended her body to the ground.[14]

Many parishes have records of usage of the churchyard for social events and local customs but none survive for St. Michael's. There is only one suggestion – that Mr. Allan of Hale Street, age unknown, told Mr.Bennitt, perhaps 64 years ago, that parish notices used to be proclaimed outside the church with the voice echoing down the valley:

'Oyeh, Oyeh Oyeh, Mr. Stephen Monkton is required to brish the hedge and clean the ditches from Barnfield stile down to the Breeches'.

The original churchyard is now owned by the Churches Conservation Trust and remains consecrated ground. Burials are restricted to those who have family connections with the church and permission must be obtained from the Diocese. The 'new' churchyard to the east is the responsibility of the Parish Council which contributes to its upkeep.

References

1. CKS U 1823/2F6.
2. CKS SD Wills Thomas Gardener 1676.
3. CKS SD Isaac Honey 1695.
4. Sharon Lawrence and Jaqueline Sergeant. Now available on Microfiche Parish Register Transcription Society. Some inscriptions were recorded with those of Hadlow by John Frost a descendant of an East Peckham family, and Librarian of New York Library. They are on open shelf in CKS. They record some otherwise unknown stones.
5. CKS U55 T650.
6. CKS P284 25/1 Papers relating to Elizabeth Anne Mitchell.
7. Curia Regis Rolls 1169–99. Robert of Stanford submits to the Grand Assize a case against Robert and Simon of Meopham with regard to a half an acre of land in Peckham as to which of them has the greater right in that piece of land.
8. BL Add Ms 34154 Rental of Eastmere Manor.
9. CKS SD Wills. Alice Stanford 1643.
10. John Stanford 1752.
11. Richard Stanford 1629.
12. CKS SD Wills Edward Martin 1695.
13. CKS SD Wills Sarah Hodge 1728.
14. CKS SD Wills Mary Featherstone 1778.

14. The Church Bells

The bells are the most mysterious aspect of the church – heard but never seen. They are housed in the tower which is 58ft 8ins to the top of the parapet externally. Within, and out of vision are six bells, now rung on special occasions by enthusiastic Kent bell ringers, but which were rung for hundreds of years by local men every Sunday as a matter of course. They were proud of their skill and served many years as recorded in the Parish Magazine in November 1915. Heading the list of long service bell ringers were 'Mr. W. Pope, 25 years and Mr. J. Saunders 20 years, T. Saunders, G.H. Bishop, H. Bishop, G. Bell, W. Honey, S. Attwood and G. Saunders.' Four of these men were still ringing 17 years later in 1932 as indicated in bold below. The longest service is that recorded in 1958 on the gravestone of 'Lewis Newman aged 80, a campanologist for 70 years'. His descendants vouch for this accuracy.

Mr. Tom Saunders was later, on March 10th 1932, to record a remarkable historic achievement. As the captain, he had been persevering for 25 years to train a band to the perfection required to ring a peal and at last he had

Figure 71. The famous St. Michael's bell ringers. Tom Saunders is fourth from left. Photograph lent by his son in 1985

Figure 72. The Church bells continue their watch in the tower. The dust of ages coats the counterweight above each bell indicating years with little inactivity.
© *David Sampson.*

succeeded. A peal consists of ringing the six bells 5040 times and every time in a different order without stopping and without making a mistake. This was the first time for about 50 years that this had been done by the church's own band of ringers without any outside help. The vicar commented:

'Ringers do not grow on every tree and it has often happened that when the team had become proficient enough to ring a peal one of the ringers will through force of circumstances leave the neighbourhood and the work of training has to be done all over again. All honour to him for his perseverance and to the entire band of ringers'.

They were: Messrs **J. Saunders, T. Saunders, H. Bishop, G.H. Bishop,** C. Saunders, E.J. Butcher, T. Warner, L. Holness.

Another memorable occasion was on 27th December 1913 when the Kent Association of Bell Ringers visited St. Michael's and gave an exhibition of change ringing lasting three hours and one minute. The record of this event hangs in the tower. They were assisted by local ringers. The ringers then *'rang out the Old and in the New Year'*. With war time conditions this could not be repeated until New Year's Eve 1918 when permission was given by the Defence of the Realm Act to ring bells after sunset. The ringers took advantage of it and assembled to carry out the old custom.

During the war another custom had to be abandoned, that of tolling a bell to announce the death of a parishioner. Mr. Donald Hodge (1894–1996), recalled that the bell tolled the number of years and workers in the field who lived in the small community would recognise who had died.

The bells were the responsibility of the Churchwardens and their accounts, which only exist from 1820, reveal that the ringers had some recompense for their exertions. They appear to have been paid an allowance of 6s.3d but it is not clear if this refers to payment or to the more likely explanation in 1834 'beer for the ringers'.

There are frequent references to renewing the bell ropes but the churchwarden's main work was the maintenance of the great bells themselves and their pride speaks from the bells. Each one is inscribed with the name of the relevant churchwarden.

The inscriptions have recently been put on a Website and are reproduced here by permission of Mr. Dickon Love for the enjoyment of many who enquire about the bells or who have had association with them and return to the church.[1] Two Jeffery sisters from Sussex visited the church in 1969 and signed the Visitor's book, 'our father used to ring the bells'.

The earliest bell is 1747. It is not known what existed in previous years. The first mention of a bell is that by Sir Roger Twysden in 1656 when his accounts record that he paid a man for tolling the bell at his wife's funeral.

The Churchwarden's accounts add numerous and interesting details to Mr. Love's work. Among them are instances of the constant care and upkeep required:

Figure 73. Bell One, showing inscriptions of the manufacturer, T. Mears and the names of the churchwardens in 1825, John Biggenden and William Allen. © David Sampson.

1827   Paid Thomas Mear's bill of £13.5s.8d for recasting a bell for the church of East Peckham.

1859   Paid Mear's the bell founder for re-hanging the bells £31.18s.6d. Tuning the organ and chiming the bells.

1891   The bells have been re-hung and recast – new bell ropes.

1936   Paid Mears and Stainbank, new clappers and fittings for the bells £34.3s. Cracked bearing £8.

The Rev Ryley speaking of the bells in the parish Magazine 1912 called them 'the artillery of the church' and quoting from George Herbert:

'Sundays observe: think when the bells do chime 'tis angels' music'.

Details of the Bells

Bell	Approx. weight	Diameter	Year cast	Founder
1	5¾ cwt (292 kg)	30" (762 mm)	1825	Thomas Mears II
2	6½ cwt (330 kg)	32½" (825 mm)	1785	William Mears
3	7½ cwt (381 kg)	35" (889 mm)	1785	William Mears
4	8⅜ cwt (425 kg)	36¾" (933 mm)	1890	Mears & Stainbank
5	10½ cwt (533 kg)	39" (991 mm)	1747	Robert Catlin
6	14 cwt (711 kg)	43" (1092 mm)	1812	Thomas Mears II

Former Bell

Bell	Approx. weight	Diameter	Year cast	Founder
4	9⅛ cwt (466 kg)	36" (914 mm)	1747	Robert Catlin

Inscriptions on the Bells

Bell	Inscription
1	T MEARS OF LONDON FECIT 1825 JOHN BIGGENDEN } CHURCHWARDENS WILLIAM ALLEN
2	W^M MEARS OF LONDON FECIT 1785 MESS^{RS} JN^O BIGGENDEN & THO^S PADDENDEN CH. WARDENS
3	W^M MEARS OF LONDON FECIT 1785 MESS^{RS} JN^O BIGGENDEN & THO^S PADDENDEN CH. WARDENS
4	
5	ROBERT CATLIN CAST AND HUNG US ALL 1747
6	THOMAS MEARS OF LONDON FECIT 1812 EDW^D MONCKTON } CHURCHWARDENS JOHN JEFFERY

Former Bell

Bell	Inscription
4	PROSPERITY TO THIS PARISH R C FECIT 1747

1747	Original 4th and present 5th cast by Robert Catlin
1785	Present 2nd and 3rd cast by William Mears
1812	Present 6th (tenor) recast by Thomas Mears II
1825	Present 1st (treble) cast by Thomas Mears II
1890	Present 4th recast by Mears and Stainbank
1907	Bells rehung by Gillett & Johnston

Reference

1 Information regarding the bells of St. Michael's obtained and reproduced from the web site of Dickon R. Love (kent.lovesguide.com).

Figure 74. Looking down from the top of the tower, the bell ropes disappear through the floor around a trap door shaped to accommodate the largest of the bells. Levers in the slotted spindle on the left would have been used along with ropes to raise and lower bells through the middle of the tower for replacement or renovation. © David Sampson.

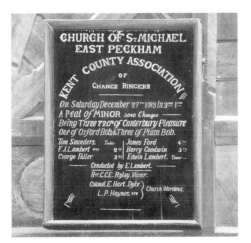

Figure 75. The narrow steps up to the bells make for a claustrophobic climb. This is the view from the top looking down. The tower is closed to visitors in the interest of safety. © David Sampson.

Figure 76. The plaque commemorating the 1913 achievement of the Kent County Association of Change Ringers is still present. © David Sampson.

15. The Church Stables

These stables are said to be unique. Standing as they do outside the churchyard wall they did not qualify for maintenance when the church building was placed in the hands of the Redundant Churches Committee in 1975.

The badly needed repairs were carried out by Lord Falmouth, as owner of the Court Lodge estate on which ground the stables stand. This fact was established in 1671 when Thomas Whetenhall, the then owner of the Court Lodge estate, wrote to Sir Roger Twysden laying claim to a small strip of bushy land joining the churchyard wall and the Court Lodge land to which Mr. Marsh the previous vicar had had no right, having caused the brush and underwood to be felled. He recorded that both he and many ancient men could remember a small tenament wherein one Crowhurst lived adjoining the churchyard wall which Sir Anthony Weldon the previous owner had caused to be pulled down because it gave disturbance by noise and tippling in time of church service.[1]

The earliest documentation for the stables is a Turnpike map of 1810, surveyed for the building of Seven Mile Lane, showing a building on the site.[2] This is followed by a note added to the Baptism register of 1797–1813 recording that the stables were enlarged by subscription about 1833. This

Figure 77. The Church stables.

date is supported by the name plates over the stalls which record the names of the village gentlemen of that time.

The building took on a new importance between 1947 and 1950 when the minutes of the Parochial Church Council record the events which led to the preservation of the stables.It was proposed that the building should be pulled down and a good shed put up in its place for the storage of tools. The meeting decided that the building was of historic interest and should be retained. It was in 1950 that it was decided that the bay reaching to the churchyard wall should be taken down and the materials used to repair the remaining section while the end nearest the church should be gabled. It is a Listed building.

Clad in weather boarding with a tiled roof it was found that the timber framing of the building is of poor quality suggesting a date of about 1800. It had been a three bay building extending north towards the churchyard wall. The foundation found under the surface gave measurements

Figure 78. The interior of the stables with name boards.

allowing for eight stalls which with the twelve in the remaining two bays accommodated twenty horses.[3] Attached to the wall plates were the name plates of the tenants.

Right	Thomas Martin	No 6	Left	William Golding	No 4
	Samuel Vine	No 17		Thomas Finch	No 5
	Sir William Bart.	No 7		Thomas Martin	No 4
	Thomas Boorman	No13/14		William Blunden	No 3
	Isaac Hatch	No 12		Cheesman	No 2
				T. Henham	

Names removed from the dilapidated bay and attached to the tier beams.[3]

Thomas Martin	16	T. H. Simmons	No 8	J. Larkin	No 2
T. Boorman	No 5	R. Starling	No 3	T. Bates	No 7
John Martyr	No 10			T.M. Wilde	No 1

From many sources the following properties have been assigned to the tenants:

No 6	Thomas Martin, Addlestead Farm
No 17	Samuel Vine, Shop keeper Hale Street
No 7	William Geary, Oxonhoath, West Peckham
No 13/14	Thomas Boorman, Medway Navigation Company
No 12	Isaac Hatch, Fant Farm
No 4	William Golding, Leavers Farm
No 5	Thomas Finch, Sand's Farm, Bullen
No 4	Thomas Martin, Hextal
No 3	William Blunden, Arnold's Lodge Farm
No 2	Cheesman, Bullen Farm
	T. Henham, Grove House or Parsonage Farm
No 16	Thomas Martin?
No 5	T Boorman
No 10	John Martyr, Miller, Branbridges
No 8	T H. Simmons, Tanner, Little Mill
No 3	R. Starling, Doctor, Vine House, Goose Green
No 2	J. Larking, Long's, (Pimms Place)
No 7	T. Bates, Miller, Little Mill
No 1	Thomas Martyr Wilde, Strettit House

In recent years the building has been frequently vandalised and the boards were taken into care by Lord Falmouth. The roofing tiles have been replaced with a modern roofing material.

References

1   U1823/2 F6.
2   QRVm 29 1810.
3   Surveyed Peter Lambert and Dawn Coster.

16. St. Michael's Schools

St. Michael's church made a substantial contribution to education at a period when the government made no grants for that purpose and such schooling as there was depended completely on voluntary effort.

St. Michael's probably associated itself with education before the end of the 18th century when Thomas Lambert, schoolmaster, was referred to in parish documents. He was probably involved either in a voluntary school for 20 boys and girls reported to the Bishop in the visitation of 1786 or in two Sunday Schools catering for 100 boys and girls of the same date. There are no accounts to ascertain who was paying but certainly by 1801 a young man, Edward Towner was paid by the Vestry *'for schooling the workhouse children'*. His 'schoolhouse', was also his home, where he ran a private school at the houses now called Coppers and Bucklers (128/130 Addlestead Road). He moved in 1812 to Pimms Cottage (132 Bush Road), where the Vestry paid him £1 for books on opening his school. It was here that the accounts show that the Vestry paid him to run a school on Sundays for those children who were employed during the week to help their family income. Here they were taught to read and write as well as being given religious education. A bill of 1818 shows an average attendance of 123 children. They were probably accommodated in a large carpenter's shed indicated in the deeds of the property.[1] The fact that the Vestry was undertaking responsibility was a positive move towards the development of education. Local concern was such that plans were made to provide a purpose built school paid for by local subscribers. Trustees were appointed. These wrote to the National Society for Promoting the Education of the Poor in the Principles of the Established Church, saying that it was their wish that their school should be united with the Society.

That Society had been founded in 1811 with the aim that the national religion should be the foundation of national education. In order to carry out this ideal they planned to establish a church school in every parish in the land in which they could communicate to the poor *'such knowledge and habits as are sufficient to guide them through life in their proper station, especially to teach them the doctrine of religion according to the practices of the established church and to train them to a performance of their religious duties by an early discipline'*. But what they also offered was financial help towards school building and it seems that by 1820 the local subscriptions were not sufficient to build a school to accommodate the number of children requiring education. Consequently for the first time the Vestry sought help from without the parish. But the help was in return for the promise that children who attended the school should also attend Divine worship on Sundays. The agreement was signed by George Moore the vicar.[2]

The Boy's National School was opened in what is now the Retreat Bungalow (291 Bullen Lane) with the Girl's school in the ground floor of the adjoining house. The children attended St. Michael's church as agreed. That school, the predecessor of the present Primary School, was later named Holy Trinity Schools when the new church and parish of Holy Trinity came into

Figure 79. Interior of St. Michael's School. Lent by a previous owner of the property.

being in 1840. The school was transferred to its present site at Chidley Cross in 1863.

In the meantime a new development had taken place. Mr. William Cook the younger, of Roydon Hall, had founded a school conducted according to the principles of the Home and Colonial Infant School Society. Founded in 1835 it was the pioneer of infant education in England. It was a purpose built school, (now a private house on Seven Mile Lane), which he allowed to be appropriated by the National Society in 1847 and bequeathed money in 1851 for its continuance as did his sister, Sophia Augusta Tarleton in 1894. The children, according to the rules of the National Society, attended St. Michael's church. With its own financial support it continued as a church school until its closure in 1946. Moreover it discontinued its association with the National Society in 1907 and became East Peckham Parochial School with the church taking increased financial responsibility. Thus the church played a caring role in the known development of education for 145 years.

The tryst with the National Society was faithfully kept and is recorded in the school Log Books[3] By 1863 the government was contributing small grants for education and required head teachers to record *'the briefest entry that will suffice to specify ordinary progress or whatever other fact concerning the school and its teachers … may require to be referred to at a future time or may otherwise deserve to be recorded'*. It was in these books that the daily routine is revealed.

The vicar attended school regularly, helping with the reading and frequently examined the children in religious knowledge. He also taught the Liturgy and taught them the Festivals of the church seasons. On other occasions he questioned them on Passion Week and the Ascension. In addition to his visits, the children left school at 10a.m. on Wednesdays and Fridays, walking to attend the 10.30am service at the church on the hill which necessarily was followed by the return walk. This involved considerable expenditure of time and energy.

According to the log book, progress was difficult owing to absenteeism.

Figure 80. Infants Class with possibly a younger Mrs. Ellis.

School attendance was not compulsory until 1880 and in the early days the teacher records that children were absent for hay making, hop tying, hop poling, harvesting, gleaning, fruiting and minding the baby.

With the arrival in 1878 of Miss Smith, who became the renowned Mrs. Ellis, the log books take on a new dimension. In a tribute at her retirement in 1920 after 42 and a third years, the Rev. Ryley said that before she came the school had been 'anyhow' but very soon her powers as a disciplinarian and influence for good began to assert themselves and chaos gave way to order and the school never looked back.

Figure 81. The Legendary Mrs. Ellis (present at St. Michael's 1878–1920) with children.

Figure 82. The Last Day at St. Michael's School. December 20th 1946. Colin Dolding (back row 3rd from right) and Joan Boyle (second row, extreme right) continue to live in the village.

In 1888 the Inspector wrote in the Log Book after examining the children in the upper and middle group;

'Great pains have been taken by the mistress to impress their minds with the moral and religious lessons taught on the history of the Old Testament and to bring out the most striking features in the life and work of our blessed Lord in the Gospels. They also showed a considerable knowledge of the meaning of words and the general plan of the Litany and answered some general questions on the catechism with fair intelligence'.

Of the infants he wrote:

'The infants answered fairly well. There were some easy questions on the usual Old and New testament narratives and some general questions on the Catechism were answered with tolerable accuracy. They seemed to lack interest and intelligence'.

It is well to remember that in the early days this was a school for girls and infants over 3 years and for boys up to 10 years which illuminates the inspector's comments!

With Mrs. Ellis's retirement the emphasis on Christian teaching continued and was frequently appraised by the inspectors. In 1935 the inspector wrote regarding religious instruction that *'I was pleased with the knowledge of the Gospel stories and the elements of Christian faith and Duty displayed by the scholars'*. General education was as thorough but it was the constant care for the children that is outstanding. In 1925 the vicar wrote in the parish magazine of his concern for them. The day after they left school children often left the village for a life 'in domestic service' where their own free time was very limited *'May I plead with parents not to delay the confirmation of their children until such time as they have left school. It frequently happens that with their schooling over children leave the parish and it is not so easy for them to come forward'*. (for confirmation)

This was a very happy school and has always been remembered with great affection by past pupils but numbers began to dwindle. At one period, 1891, there had been 70 children on register with an average attendance of 62 but by 1945 the number had dropped to 23.

In May 1945 the head teacher received an official letter from the Ministry of Education concerning *'a proposal to cease to maintain this school'*. The last day was December 20th 1946 when a photograph was taken (Fig. 82) recording the end of St. Michael's work in education. The entry in the Log Book reads: *'St. Michael's School closed for good.'*

References

1   CKS U47/17 T66 Includes the reference 'to erect a carpenter's shop'. There is evidence in the village of another 'schoolroom' held in a shed.

2   See Margaret Lawrence. Peckham Pupils. The Development of Education in a Kentish Village.

3   CKS C/ES 284/1 St. Michael's School Log Book.

17. The Foundlings

The gallery at the west end of the Georgian church to seat the children was used by many children who are not to be found in the baptism records because they were not born in East Peckham. A number of them seated there had been given birth under difficult conditions and were baptised the Sunday following their admission to the Foundling Hospital in London which cared for the maintenance and education of deserted and exposed young children. This had been founded by the benevolent sea captain, Thomas Coram, in 1740. He had been enraged at the sight of unwanted babies thrown on dung heaps. At baptism the children were given a number which always remained attached to them. They were then sent to country districts around London for wet nursing. East Peckham was one of the many areas originally chosen but eventually by 1808 the hospital only retained our parish and one other place, Chertsey in Surrey, for this purpose. The hospital kept meticulous records of each child, many of whom such as John Lambourne, Foundling No.11504, buried at St. Michael's, in 1759 died in infancy while others grew to be 'fine healthy children'.

They were supervised by a Superintendent who made regular reports to the hospital. Some idea of the numbers involved can be assumed from a later report, in 1807, by Mr. John Vine, the local doctor and Inspector, who described 54 children – 40 were in good health, 4 had whooping cough, 6 weakly, 2 with scrophula, 1 an idiot, 1 with fits. Later information gives much higher numbers.

The women were paid by the hospital for the children's upkeep, 3s 6d a week plus £4.4s a year for clothing, but it was found in 1836 that even the oldest nurses of forty years could not remember any money being paid to them. It appears to have been a general understanding that the Inspector of the Kent District who kept a hucksters shop paid all the nurses under his charge in goods furnished from his shop on Hale Street. (Now Orchard Court) There was no reflection on the honesty and integrity of Mr. Hatch, the inspector. The neighbours spoke in the highest terms of his integrity and fair dealing; his aim was to

Figure 83. Thomas Coram. He was the inspiration for the Foundling Hospital. Window in the church porch of Lyme Regis, his home town (author's photograph).

Figure 84. Foundling children in nineteenth century dress. From a postcard treasured by many foundings.

prevent the nurses' husbands squandering the money in drink.

The women who fostered the children in their own homes established a tradition which continued for many years of which memories and associations linger to the present day. Very prominent is 'Brunswick Square' a property in Pound Road. Mr Fred Hodge owned a run down property known as 'The Square'. This had a bad reputation and he wished to rename it when the site was re built in 1936. Having an adopted daughter, a foundling, he renamed it with the address of the Foundling Hospital in London.

How many children were fostered in East Peckham up to 1885, after which records remain closed, could only be counted by many hours spent with the records at The Metropolitan Archives but the number, over a possible two hundred years to within living memory, must be thousands. They are recorded on the Censuses of the Population which required place of birth to be entered. A foundling's place of birth is registered as 'unknown' but in many cases when they returned to East Peckham they married and raised their own families. Martha Gedney aged 2 years on the 1901 census living at Brook Farm Cottages has her great grandchildren living in the village. Her daughter cherishes the postcard of the Coram children wearing their uniform.

Another living memory to hand is that of Mrs. Eva Wenham whose grandmother Mrs. Stevens died aged 80 in 1960 having reared twenty foundlings. She lived at what is now Coppers and Bucklers at Addlestead Road. After her death one of those foundlings paid a tribute to her in verse.

The Late Mrs. Stevens of East Peckham

Her face was sweet and kindly
Her heart was more than gold
As twenty babes she fondled
Could willingly have told.

Unlike the woman in the shoe
She knew exactly what to do
She worked and toiled like many another
To earn the name of a good mother.

Happy days were spent
In her cottage down in Kent
Till that sad and dreary day
When our dear mother passed away.

I like to think that when she died
The gates of Heaven were opened wide
That Thomas Coram and St. Peter
Came down the heavenly steps to meet her.

And led her to the judgement seat
To hear her Lord and King repeat
In voice so strong and fervent
Well done thou good and faithful servant.

(L. Hampson, born Wigram)

Another memory is that of Mrs Maire Elizabeth Owen, who was born to an unmarried mother in 1926 and was given to Coram Hospital shortly after. She was placed at two months old in the home of the Pope family at No 1 The Freehold, East Peckham. She vividly recalls her happy childhood there and the day it all came to an end.

Her account emphasises the bond with her Mother, her Dad and her family, including the wonderful big, big brother Bill and other foundlings who she regarded as her foster brothers and sisters. This bonding was characteristic of the 'Foundling experience'.

Her happy life was associated with the hop picking.

'One misty damp September morning, I was walking by and holding on to a high black pram. In the pram was my baby brother George. Piled on top of him so that only his little face could be seen, were pots, pans, thermos flasks, tins of food and all the paraphernalia needed for a family picnicking for the day. Mother was pushing the pram, we were one of the many families heading for the hop gardens and once the 'Hoppers Mist' lifted we would enjoy a lovely summer's day. While the work was going on the children would run around, shouting, playing watching carefully not to be trampled on by the beautiful huge shire horses that pulled the large, wooden-wheeled carts laden with hops, on their way to be dried in the strange shaped oast houses. The tally men, (the men who graded the hops and decided the price per bushel to be paid to the pickers) would often toss a child into a full bin of hops. The memory of the women in their sack aprons, long dresses and large hats, laughing at the happy screams of the child and the other children shouting, 'Me next, me next', brings a smile to my lips as I write. Half way through the day, we would sit around the bins having dinner of cheese, buttered rolls, tomatoes, and sometimes the men gave us hot potatoes that had been baked in the ashes of the oast house fires'.

But above all the laughter and shouts was the feeling of being hugged onto a rough apron, the love of her mother and aunt and the happiness of a child's freedom, of running round and round, sleeping on the ground and riding home on the pram, her little legs clad in woollen socks and buttoned boots banging over the side and little George asleep on his pillow of hops.

But it was in that happy atmosphere of the hop garden that she had the first sign that her happy life would end. A man, the village doctor who had responsibility for the foundlings, *'came and talked to my mother and she cried. I hugged her sack aproned body and childlike cried with her as she patted my head. Soon after this day, a few children stood with parents and other relatives at the Pound bus stop. A charabanc came and I was so excited as Bill lifted me in, giving me his lunch case, full of monkey nuts; how could we children know that day was to bring so many tears and changes. I turned to wave at Bill, I saw him place his arm round Mother's shoulders. Was she also thinking, and perhaps seeing the future, and was she crying? If I could have known what was happening or could have foreseen the future, nobody would have torn me away from my beloved brother. It was twelve years before I saw him again'.*

Although she writes of this sad day she also remembers that she had a wonderful upbringing at the Foundling Hospital Schools. She says that while it was customary for the children to return to the Foundling Hospital School at five years old they maintained their links with their home because the mothers would go to London on a charabanc to visit their children and the children would return for holidays. Now living in Yorkshire she re-lives her life as a foundling by speaking to groups of people.

Such was the children's attachment to East Peckham that when Walter Ady was killed in the Second World War serving with the Middle East Expeditionary Force, his papers claimed that his home was with his foster parents on Hale Street and his name is on the Holy Trinity war memorial.

More recent memories are recalled by Mr. Bunt, himself a foundling. He remembers that the foundlings stopped coming in 1952 and notes how many returned and married.

The Foundling Museum opened June 2004 at 40 Brunswick Square, London but East Peckham has its own 'museum'.[1]

Reference
1 All records of the Thomas Coram Hospital have been deposited at the London Metropolitan Archives. Records since 1885 containing personal information about named individuals remain closed for 110 years. The Coram Family undertakes to give counselling and advice to relatives of former foundlings.

18. The Church Today

St. Michael's was vested in the care of the Redundant Churches Fund later more positively renamed The Churches Conservation Trust. A handsome plaque outside the church testifies to this and inside a notice reminds the visitor that this is a place for reflection and calm. This is a fact well recognised by local people and by the numerous walkers who traverse the footpath sign – posted 'The Greensand Way' which passes through the churchyard.

Repairs have been speedily carried out. Owing to a regrettable incident of arson in 1994, too shameful to record, the damaged pews from the south aisle were removed and the floor space tiled. This leaves a useful space for exhibitions and refreshments.

In recent years the church has been open on Heritage Weekends attracting hundreds of visitors drawn by this ancient and remote building. Staffed by volunteers arrangement have been made since 2003 to open the church on Sunday afternoons in the summer months from April to September. The Patronal Festival service is held in September as near as possible to St. Michael's Day, 30th September.

Figure 85. The Church today. Conserved by the Churches Conservation Trust. © Colin Rainer.

19. Reflection and Epilogue

Although the closure of the church can be superficially attributed to modern conditions much deeper social trends contributed.

It was in fact the culmination of a long, slow isolation of the church which began in 1835 with the passing of the New Poor Law which relieved the Parish Vestry of their centuries old responsibility for the poor. This meant that the church was no longer the centre for social care. Although the Vestry continued for some time with their other responsibilities the gradual introduction of State administration led to a hopeless muddle of church and civil duties. This was at last sorted with the passing of the Parish Council Act in 1894 when civic duties were passed to the new Parish Council leaving the church for the first time merely responsible for its spiritual duties. This had the side effect that the Churchwardens could no longer raise an assessment for *'the necessary reparations and other expenses in and belonging to the parish church of East Peckham'*. Objected to by many, especially non conformists, the cost of maintenance was removed from the voting public. Now the financial responsibility lay solely with the church going congregation.

Furthermore the Visitation records, already referred to, state that there were only fourteen houses of any note in the parish. These were the larger farm houses such as Forge Farm, Leavers, Goose Green, Crowhurst, Hextall Court, Peckham Place, Grove Farm, Pond Farm, Mount Pleasant, Parsonage (then Little Roydon) and Roydon Hall. Eventually, as farming began to fail these houses were taken by professional people such as Colonels and Admirals who contributed generously to the upkeep of the church. When society changed again the church missed their financial support. Admiral Chapman and the Hon. Mrs. Chapman moved from Little Roydon in 1920 after 16 years, Colonel Hart Dyke moved from Leavers in 1925 after 21 years, Mr. and Mrs. Elvins moved from Grove House after 17 years, Colonel Moreland and the Hon Mrs. Moreland from Hextall in 1921 after 15 years. In fact the Rev. Ryley remarked in 1927 that in the 16 years he had been there only ten houses, (including cottages) had not changed hands. The limited means of the small population could not match their love, devotion and service to the church. The gradual mechanisation on the farm and, further, the decline of the hop industry resulted in fewer labourers and consequently fewer children which led to the closure of the church school.

These social changes at St. Michael's were the product of a comparatively recent period in its history. Equally profound changes had taken place over the centuries. The Manor of East Peckham has long ceased to exist as have the ancient land units of the Hundreds of Littlefield and Twyford which bisected the village. Also archaic are the 'Boroughs' into which the parish had once been divided, Upper Borough, Lone Borough and Stockenbury, which are now meaningless except to historians. These secular units for administering public order, justice and taxation did not endure. But the unit which imposed itself on the unfolding medieval community was the Parish, the area of land in which the people lived who came under the spiritual care of the appointed clergyman. This shows the enduring influence of the church in our society. What has survived into yet another century despite the closure of its representative building, St. Michael's church, is the Parish now concealed under the name of Holy Trinity.

This is the story of St. Michael's Church, East Peckham - Parish and People as at July 1st 2004.

~

At the time of the closure of St. Michael's church the language of the 1662 Book of Common Prayer was under scrutiny. Changes which were in process then have since come to pass with most churches now using a modern idiom. But the old words which had resounded for over three hundred years, spoken by men of women of many different persuasions, are those best fitted to form an epilogue to this long story.

The imperfections of the past are acknowledged in the words of the General Confession:

Almighty and most merciful Father we have erred and strayed from thy ways like lost sheep, we have followed too much the devises and desires of our own hearts, we have offended against thy holy laws. We have left undone those things which we ought to have done and we have done those things which we ought not to have done and there is no health in us. But thou O Lord have mercy upon us miserable offenders, spare thou them O God which confess their faults; restore thou them that are penitent according to thy promises declared unto mankind in Christ Jesus our Lord. And grant, most merciful Father for his sake that we may hereafter live a godly righteous and sober life to the glory of thy holy Name.

The assurance of the future is anticipated by extracts from a well known hymn from which the title of this history was taken:

For all the saints who from their labours rest,
Who thee by faith before the world confessed,
Thy name O Jesus be for ever blessed. Alleluya.

But lo, there breaks a yet more glorious day;
The saints triumphant rise in bright array;
The King of Glory passes on his way. Alleluya.

From earth's wide bounds from ocean's farthest coast,
Through gates of pearl streams in the countless host,
Singing to Father, Son and Holy Ghost. Alleluya.

Bibliography

I recommend the following books which I have consulted and enjoyed.

Bettey, J.H. **Church and Parish.** Batsford 1987.

Burgess, F. **English Churchyard Memorials.** SPCK 1963.

Clark, P. **English Provincial Society from Reformation to Revolution 1540–1640.** Harvester Press 1977.

Cook, A. **A Manor Through Four Centuries.** Oxford 1938.

Dickens, A.G. **The English Reformation.** Collins 1967.

Dudley-Ward, C.H. **The Family of Twysden and Twisden.** Murray 1939.

Duffy, E. **The Stripping of the Altars. Traditional Religion in England 1400–1580.** Yale University Press 1992.

Garrett, C.H. **The Marian Exiles.** Cambridge University Press 1936.

Harrington, Pearson and Rose. **The Kent Hearth Tax Assessment. Lady Day 1665.** British Record Society and Kent Archaeological Society 2000.

Jessup, F.W. **Sir Roger Twysden.** Cresset Press 1965.

Pearson, S. **Medieval Houses of Kent. An Historical Analysis.** RCHM 1994.

Thirsk, J. **Alternative Agriculture. A History From the Black Death to the Present Day.** Oxford 1997.

Thompson, J. **The Later Lollards.** Oxford 1965.

Yates, Hume and Hastings. **Religion and Society in Kent 1640–1914.** Boydell Press and Kent County Council 1994.

Witney, K. **The Jutish Forest.** Athlone Press 1976.

Zell, M. **Industry in the Countryside. Wealden Society in the 16th Century.** Cambridge University Press 1996.

Zell, M. Edited. **Early Modern Kent 1540–1640.** Boydell Press and Kent County Council 2000.

By the same author.

Through This Door. St. Michaels Church, East Peckham. 1974.

Peckham Pupils. The Development of Education in a Kentish Village. 1979. Kent County Library.

The New Church. Holy Trinity Church, East Peckham 1840 Onwards. 1988.

The Bridge Over the Stream. The History of the Parish Council 1894–1994. 1997.

The Encircling Hop. A History of the Hop and Brewing Industry. 1994. Sawd Publications.

Index

Figure 86. Royal Coat of Arms 1740. © Colin Rainer.

Whetenhall;